The Sinking of the Bismarck

Titles in the 'Fortunes of War' series

FORTUNES OF WAR

The Sinking of the Bismarck

WILL BERTHOLD

TRANSLATED FROM THE GERMAN
BY MICHAEL BULLOCK

CERBERUS

First published in the UK by Longmans, Green & Co., Limited in 1958

PUBLISHED IN THE UNITED KINGDOM BY;
Cerberus Publishing Limited
22A Osprey Court
Hawkfield Business Park
Bristol BS14 0BB
UK
Tel: +44 (0) 1275 54 54 70
Fax: +44 (0) 1275 54 54 72
e–mail: cerberusbooks@aol.com
www.cerberus–publishing.com

© Cerberus Publishing Ltd 2004

British Library Cataloguing in Publication Data.
A catalogue record for this book is available from the British Library.

ISBN 1 84145 037 5

PRINTED AND BOUND IN ENGLAND.

Introduction

When the *Bismarck* was sighted off Bergen, the news of her sailing quickly reached the Admiralty. The German squadron was intercepted in the Denmark strait. In the first bitter engagement HMS *Hood*, the pride of the Royal Navy, was blown-up and the new battleship HMS *Prince of Wales* damaged. From the moment of that disastrous first action it became a crucial call on the Royal Navy to destroy the German battleship.

In this book, told from the point of view of the crew of the *Bismarck*, is described the hunt and the final kill; the end is a horrific portrayal of defeat at sea.

Berthold tells this great and exciting story in human terms; he depicts the fears and courage of the crew as the end slowly, inevitably approaches; he recreates the thoughts of home that accompanied the sailors to their deaths; he speaks against the futility of all warfare.

There will be few who will not be enthralled and moved by this vivid account of a great naval action seen, in this book, from the side of the defeated enemy.

THE SINKING OF THE *BISMARCK*

The 'wire' had been 'buzzing' for hours. When the first trail of evening mist drifted past the slender colossus, the Admiral came aboard. Now everyone knew the matter was serious. Things were moving. Into the war. To the naval front. To the British-dominated Atlantic. All leave cancelled as from now. The harbour sweethearts and the officers' wives and the mothers of the young sailors would wait in vain today.

The engagement began with stew. The gangplank still linked the flagship *Bismarck* to the land that 2,287 of her crew would never see again. A week later that number would be ripped to pieces by shells, shattered by torpedoes, crushed by bombs, or drowned in puddles of blazing oil on the swirling sea.

But none of those who now tucked hungrily into their stew were thinking of that. Who thinks of dying, while he is still in port?

The men on board played cards. They listened to the radio. They told one another crude jokes and laughed at them. Others were more serious, they wrote to their mothers, their sweethearts, their wives. They were restless, but confident. Confidence was catching. Confidence was called for. Confidence was an order. Confidence was a matter of course when you were aboard the most modern battleship in the world. It radiated from the ice-grey, steely cold 15-inch guns, l75,000-h.p. turbines, the 190,000 shells in the giant ship's armoured magazines.

The sailors knew that enemy projectiles would first have to bite through impenetrable nickel-chrome-steel plates, such as no other ship in the world but the *Bismarck* possessed; they knew their ship couldn't sink, that during the last months of the working-up and the trials in the Baltic every manipulation, every manoeuvre, every eventuality had been tried out hundreds and thousands of times.

There was nothing the 45,000-ton *Bismarck* had to fear – nothing save what was to come....

Four of the crew were still missing – Sub-Lieutenant Peters and three men detailed to the hydrographical survey office. Their job was to enter the most recently established mine-free routes in the *Bismarck*'s charts. They finished this during the afternoon. Since they were not expected back on board till later, they decided to make the best of their few hours' leisure.

They stopped a lorry and hitch-hiked from Gotenhafen to Danzig, where there were dear drinks and cheap girls. They drove along roads lined with rich green chestnuts and flowering cherry trees. But they didn't see the spring. They weren't interested in the beauty of the May day. They wanted a last taste of land, or what a sailer understands by land.

The lorry stopped outside an inn. They gave the driver a few cigarettes and were in a hurry to be off.

'Be here by nineteen hours,' said the Sub-Lieutenant. 'Otherwise there'll be hell to pay.'

'Aye-aye, sir,' responded the three men. Then they went off laughing...

Only the typical sound of a ship, the low, regular hum and whirr of the auxiliary machinery, showed that the *Bismarck* would soon be towed out of the harbour by tugs. The crew no longer noticed the monotonous drone. During the last few hours they had been reinforced by 300 'holiday-makers'; this was the name they gave to the 82-man staff of the Fleet Commander, Admiral Lütjens, and the crews of the five naval aircraft, who were permanently off watch until things began to hot up.

The flagship *Bismarck* was a floating town with neighbours who knew one another, and strangers who had never met and passed each other without a word, with squares and streets, barbers' saloons, laundries, shoemakers' and tailors' workshops. Only when the ship was in action were the barbers, cobblers, tailors, civilian stewards and canteen managers subject to naval discipline as medical orderlies. Superiors were saluted only once a day.

There were, of course, no women on this 1,140-foot-long, 118-foot-wide floating town. Women appeared only in the shape of photographs with faces wreathed in frozen smiles or rigidly grave, respectable buttoned well up to the neck, or half-naked pin-ups, pasted on the lockers, between the bunks or on the steel bulkheads. These photos were the common property of the crew and permanent topic number one.

The Fleet Commander ordered five officers into the chart-room. He had a narrow, sour face and short hair meticulously parted. He spoke 'High German' free of any local accent and eyed his officers, among them the Commander, Captain Lindemann, without a trace of personal sympathy.

'Gentlemen,' he began, 'we put to sea in two hours. To disguise our departure our sister ship, the *Tirpitz*, will berth here tonight. We enter Norwegian waters tomorrow morning, refuel quickly at Bergen and then join forces with the *Prinz Eugen*, which will operate along with us. Our job is to attack merchant shipping in the Atlantic. Orders from the Supreme Naval Command are to avoid clashes with enemy warships as far as possible.'

The Admiral looked up for a moment from the chart table. His face still wore its sour look. His snow-white collar was a shade too wide. Between the corners hung the Knight's Cross.

'We may assume that the enemy will spot the *Bismarck*'s entry into the conflict while we are still in Norway. We shall put out from Bergen with a fake convoy and then carry on alone with the *Prinz Eugen*. All available German U-boats are in the proposed area of operations and the *Luftwaffe* is also intensifying its activities. Supply ships are standing by at points arranged by myself. Any questions?'

'No, sir,' replied Captain Lindemann.

'Good... I have no doubt that the enemy are fully informed as to the *Bismarck*'s fire-power and range of action. They will throw in everything they've got. We shall either return victorious or not at all.'

The Admiral dismissed his officers with a brief nod. He looked through them as though they were made of glass. He was not a man to their taste. But they were far too deeply rooted in the tradition of the German Navy to admit it.

It was easier for the crew. They unhesitatingly nick-named Fleet Commander Günther Lütjens the 'Black Devil'.

Sub-Lieutenant Peters was first at the rendezvous. He was small, thin and pale. A quarter of an hour ago he had said goodbye to his mother. He didn't tell her the *Bismarck* was putting to sea, but she knew, she could feel it, and she cried. He was annoyed by her tears and angry because they cut him to the quick. He shook the thought of the old lady abruptly from him, cursed his three men for being late and felt he could do with a drink.

The second to arrive was Able Seaman Pfeiffer, a lad of barely eighteen, who preferred war to school. For the moment at least.

'Had a good time?' asked Peters.

'Yes, sir.'

'Where are the others?'

'I don't know. I went off on my own.'

'Why?'

'I didn't feel like going with them. It's always the same... You didn't go with them either, sir.'

'If those two don't come now, we're sunk.'

The Sub-Lieutenant was already regretting his trip to Danzig. Beside him, on the inn bench, lay the charts the Navigating Officer was urgently waiting for. He thought of his mother and looked at his wrist-watch.

At that moment the two Petty Officers appeared. Mehring was saying in a thick voice, 'Now we've got to get back on the steamer.' Hinrichs didn't look much better. He was red in the face and kept belching.

'Devil take you,' said Peters.

'Very good, Admiral,' replied Mehring. 'The devil can take us all later. But now it's time to get going. Our car is waiting outside.'

The Sub-Lieutenant stopped short when he saw the car. A black box of a vehicle with a silver palm branch – in the front. The two Petty Officers had 'organized' a hearse.

'Very symbolic,' said Able Seaman Pfeiffer.

'Shut your trap,' exclaimed Hinrichs. 'Hearses bring luck.'

The four mariners stood bent among branches of artificial evergreens and faded ribbons. They held on to the coffin handles. The unaccustomed surroundings momentarily damped their conversation.

At every curve in the road they fell against one another, cursing and laughing. Mehring took a bottle of spirits from under his tunic, drew the cork and held it out to Peters.

'Cheers,' he said. 'Better drink than drown.'

The bottle passed from mouth to mouth. Peters, who couldn't take drink at all, felt the spirits go straight to his head. Mehring was bawling a song. Pfeiffer drank unwillingly with a sour face.

'Where did you get to?' asked Hinrichs.

'Mind your own business.'

'Man,' rejoined the Petty Officer, 'I believe he went to church. I hope you prayed for us as well.'

The bottle went round again.

'Would you like to know where we went?' asked Mehring.

'We all know where you were,' answered Peters. 'In the whore-house, of course.'

'The proper place for a sailor.'

Mehring belched and then went on : 'We did it for you, too.'

The bottle was now almost empty. Pfeiffer had lost his aversion to the cheap liquor and was swilling it down. Peters was almost tight. The two Petty Officers had long passed the Plimsoll line.

'I'd like to know what you two came to Danzig for,' Mehring started off again. 'Man, I went straight for a red-head. I thought she was the one. Not worth a straw. It cost ten marks. Then I grabbed the blonde, you know, the one with a good heart. Hot stuff, I can tell you. That's always the way, the blondes keep the promises made by the red-heads. How did you get on?'

He jabbed his elbow in Hinrichs's ribs. But Hinrichs was miles away, still bawling his song.

'He'll be sick in a minute.'

'Pull yourselves together,' said Peters. 'Here we are.'

'Pull yourself together, Sub-Lieutenant. You're the one who's got to report.'

The hearse had reached its destination, it drove along the quayside and came to a stop. It was rather misty, visibility thirty or forty yards perhaps.

'Well, where's our boat?' asked Mehring. He gave the driver some cigarettes. 'If you drive like that again,' he told him, 'you'll have the coffin lid overboard, chum.'

The Sub-Lieutenant held the rolled-up charts tight under his arm. The fresh air nearly bowled him over. The car turned round and drove off.

'Am I drunk?' asked Peters. "The ship's gone!'

The *Bismarck* had left her berth. She was lying in the roads. It took the Sub-Lieutenant and his men half an hour to find this out. Time was now getting very short. A launch took them out to the flagship. They clambered up the accommodation ladder. Hinrichs trod on Pfeiffer's hand. Pfeiffer swore. A full bottle of liquor fell out of Mehring's tunic.

'Hell,' he said.

Peters was the first to reach the deck. Five yards away stood Lieutenant-Commander Werner Nobis. Peters went up to him and saluted. 'Sub-Lieutenant Peters and three men reporting back from the hydrographical survey office,' he announced;

'Drunk?' answered Nobis.

'No, sir.'

'Go away and eat coffee beans, man. My watch will be over in half an hour, bring me the charts then. Sober. Understand?'

'Yes, sir.'

Mehring, Hinrichs and Pfeiffer slipped away quickly.

'I don't know whether I'm coming or going,' ex-claimed Mehring. 'And now the booze has gone west too.... Good luck to it. ... But now I'm going to pitch the lads a yarn.'

Half an hour later the *Bismarck* weighed anchor and put to sea, shaping a course through the Great Belt to Skagerrak. The main engines were now running. The vibration could be felt only on A Bridge and below. The order was given to stand down. The watch below were told to sleep and save their energy for the coming action. But for most of the young sailors it was their first sortie against the enemy, and they expected something to happen at any moment.

Everyone was in excellent spirits. They were almost all volunteers, youngsters who had not yet gained or lost anything by the war. The war of 1941, when everything seemed set for a German victory... Calmly and proudly the flagship ploughed through the waves. She had a speed of 28 knots, which could be increased to 31 knots at maximum pressure. Her draught was 33 feet when fully loaded. Then she had a displacement of 45,000 tons. From the water-line to the masthead she was 72 feet high. The outer skin had the additional protection of a strong nickel-chrome-steel torpedo belt. No British torpedo of the year 1941 was powerful enough to smash through this wall.

Eighty-nine guns of all calibres waited for the enemy. The four turrets were equipped with hydraulically loaded twin barrels 15 inches in diameter. The diameter was nothing, for the German Navy had fired from the same calibre in World War I. The new factor was that the *Bismarck*'s guns could be aimed to within a few feet in pitch darkness by radar.

There were fire control posts in the tops, forward and aft, and in the conning positions. Half a division, about 60 men, slept on each of the mess decks, which were situated as close as possible to the fire control posts. The officers slept in twos. Only the Commanding Officer, the Fleet Commander and the Executive Officer had single cabins.

Below decks it was as clean, quiet and tidy as a hospital. The ship was heated by her own boilers. The temperature was automatically regulated. The *Bismarck* took five years to build and cost £30 million. No significant constructional fault could be detected during the months of trials. Nor when she went into action.

Nor after she had been sunk....

On the deck occupied by the Second Engine-Room Half-Division no one was asleep. The men had been off watch for two hours. If there was no air raid warning they would have another six hours. Not much had happened today. Moessmer was caught smoking and told to do patrol on the upper deck as a punishment. A Lieutenant thundered the order at him. Moessmer ran a hundred yards, jumped through a hatch and disappeared. The officer didn't know him and Moessmer didn't know the officer; there was no better hiding-place in the whole world than the *Bismarck*.

Hengst was ordered to report to Lieutenant-Commander Bilk. He spent three hours looking for the officers' mess and asked twenty of his companions, but none of them could give him any idea where it was. He tried to get in touch with it by telephone, but was told that all the lines were engaged by official calls. By the time he found the Lieutenant-Commander, the officer had forgotten what he wanted him for, and the AB came away with a flea in his ear.

Burger had a belly-ache. He stuck it for two hours and then reported to the sick-bay. He was suffering from acute appendicitis and before he knew what had happened, the AB found himself lying on the operating-table, already anaesthetized. While still under the ether mask, he cursed because he was afraid he would sleep through the first engagement. The operation went off without complications.

Then Lauchs announced that he had seen one of the civilian stewards knocking off a crate of brandy. Suddenly they were all thirsty. They remembered that Petty Officer Lindenberg had been a locksmith in civilian life. They let him into the plot and he manufactured a picklock. The civilian stewards were the only ones who had locked their cupboards. The picklock worked perfectly. But they didn't find the brandy till they came to the sixth locker. They crept soundlessly back to their own deck and closed the bulkheads. They couldn't prevent Petty Officer Lindenberg's pals from joining in the drinking. But at least this meant they had nothing to fear from the petty officers...

A lookout was posted in the passage and changed at intervals. After the first two bottles had been drunk, the current lookout was forgotten. He came in, protesting thirstily. They withdrew their observation posts. From now on they didn't give a damn about anything. They knew by experience that at this time of day the officers rarely appeared on a mess deck, and petty officers could be bribed with brandy. Apart from a few spoil-sports. But they were in other sections of the ship.

This was how the first sortie began for the Second Engine-Room Half-Division. They fraternized with the drunken petty officers. In action or during a booze-up petty officers could be smashing chaps. It was months now since the time when the *Bismarck*'s cubs were still being licked into shape on the barrack square.

Again and again they drank to Leading Seaman Link. He was getting married in seven days. Since they didn't know whether they would have any brandy left by then, or time to drink it, they were celebrating his marriage by proxy in advance.

'What's her name?' inquired Lindenberg.

'Else.'

'Show me a snap.'

Link readily handed it round.

'She's got a pretty face,' stated a petty officer in the tones of a connoisseur.

'To your wedding,' shouted the chorus.

Damned good fun, this war. Like being in a sleeping carriage. Waiter, another brandy, please. The old tub was well heated. Best-quality drinks, top-hole grub. Top-notch petty officers who drank like fishes. A smashing bunch of officers who were always asleep when they weren't on duty. Super ship, you didn't even feel sea-sick. Not for the moment, anyhow.... They drank to everything in turn. Last of all to the war at sea.

'How long have you been in the Navy?' someone asked Lindenberg.

'Three years.'

'Where did you pick up your Iron Cross?'

'In a minesweeper.'

'What did you get it for?'

'Two Iron Crosses had been allotted to us. Then the tub went to the bottom, and I was one of the only two left alive.'

'How did it go down?'

'Hit a mine. The keel ran right on to it. I happened to be aft.'

"What about the others?'

'They weren't aft... Cheer up, no need to turn pale. Mines can't hurt us.'

'Where else have you been?'

'In a supply ship,' answered Lindenberg. All at once the effects of the alcohol wore off. He looked pale and pinched. It infected the others. Everyone's high spirits left them.

'That's the lousy thing about war at sea. You sit there waiting for some big tub like the *Bismarck* to come along. But it doesn't come. Instead the Tommies arrive with their planes and plaster you to their hearts' content. You've got a few guns, it's true, but the airmen can drop their bombs from such a height that your shells don't even reach them. If a bomb hits the ship, it goes up in flames. A first-class cremation.... No need to turn pale, you lot. You're not on a tanker... You've got all the luck. We're in clover here.'

The petty officer didn't feel like drinking any more. He said good-night, stood up and left. The others, too, now turned away from the brandy.

Link had long ago crawled into his cubicle. He shut his eyes. He saw Else before him. The girl he loved. Slim, blonde Else with the childlike eyes who in seven days, at 10.30 a.m., would stand alone in the registry office. And would be a widow before she ever became a wife.

But she didn't know that. Link didn't know it either.

The smoke got in his eyes. Tears welled up. On the table stood an open bottle of brandy in which nobody was any longer interested. Link climbed out of his bunk again and put the bottle to bis lips. If he hit the pillow again at once he would have three hours to sleep.

He knew nothing of his fate. No one on the *Bismarck* knew, suspected or felt what was in store. The gloomiest imagination could not picture what awaited the flagship of the German fleet.

Leading Seaman Herbert Link merely had his head ripped off by a shell. That was a comparatively merciful fate....

When the cold mists of morning raised the curtain on the coming day, 20 May, 1941, the *Bismarck*, surrounded by destroyers and minesweepers and escorted by aircraft, was at exactly the predetermined point. Captain Lindemann, the wiry officer whom his crew adored, was still commanding his ship. He would not hand over to Admiral Lütjens until after the *Bismarck* had joined up with the *Prinz Eugen*.

The first contacts with enemy aircraft or submarines were now possible. But they did not take place. Nor did anything happen hours later, when the *Bismarck* steamed into Norwegian waters.

Operation *Bismarck* had been prepared with un-paralleled thoroughness. The Commander-in-Chief of Northern Command transferred infantry units to Bergen and assembled divisions in the port. Fake convoys sailed up and down the coast. Landing craft prepared for action. The second, fifth and seventh mine-sweeper fleets kept ceaseless check on the mine-free routes 'Agathe' and 'Dorothea'. The chain of outposts of the Naval Commander-in-Chief, Norway, advanced to the ice barrier. German spotter planes were continually in the air.

All these measures were intended to confuse the enemy. He was not to know whether the *Bismarck* was supporting a German invasion of Iceland, whether she was escorting a mammoth convoy, or whether she was breaking through into the Atlantic, more or less on her own, to harry merchant shipping.

The Norwegian agents of the British passed on to London the facts as they saw them with their own eyes. They had no idea that the German security forces were intercepting every one of their reports. Canaris's people had known all about the major network of Norwegian agents for months and had planted their own representatives in it. But they were postponing the destruction of this organization until the day the *Bismarck* steamed out to meet the enemy for the first time.

The flagship of the German fleet reached Bergen around noon, under a radiant blue sky and on a calm sea. Those of the crew not on watch were sunning themselves on deck. Ashore, German soldiers were congregating and waving to the ship. One of them got hold of a boat, rowed out to the *Bismarck* and shouted to the upper deck: 'Got any fags?'

The sailors laughed and threw the enterprising oarsman whole packages of cigarettes.

The corporal waved up to them, laughed and shouted: 'Next war I'll join the Navy.'

There were other attractions ashore. Two tall blonde Norwegian girls strolled along the quay, followed by the hungry eyes of the soldiers. Every now and then they stopped and laughed over to the men.

'What a nice ship. What's she called?' one of the girls asked an NCO.

'I don't know,' he replied. 'But she's certainly a beauty.'

The two girls had no idea that today their movements were also being watched by eyes in no way concerned with their feminine charms. That the security forces were on their heels, that everything they did was noted. That the men who were following them knew exactly where they would go. That their destination was already surrounded. That these men were only waiting for one more radio message to be sent out before arresting them.

The girls went back to Ame, to Arne Svjenrod, who with his left hand supplied the German Navy with dried cod, while with the right he tapped out Morse messages to London. They told him what they had seen. He couldn't make much of their report. The British were sending through urgent requests for the vessel's armament, tonnage and radius of action. At Scapa Flow they were still uncertain whether it was the *Bismarck*. According to the British Admiralty's calculations the *Bismarck* wouldn't be ready for action for another two months.

The British didn't know that her trials had been cut short.

Arne went down to the harbour himself. First of all in connexion with dried cod. He informed the naval authorities of the arrival of a fresh consignment. Then he strolled along the beach. One of many attracted by the fine weather and curiosity. He noted four gun turrets. His eyes were practised. He estimated the tonnage more or less correctly. And he came to the conclusion that it must be the *Bismarck* or the *Tirpitz* on whose deck the sailors were sunning themselves. He saw she was refuelling. He observed the preparations for putting to sea.

All of a sudden he was in a hurry. He went back to his office, quickly left it, entered an outbuilding, a back room, took a box down from the wall, removed an oil-cloth and set to on the tapper.

They were already waiting for his call. He radioed:

'German battleship, probably *Bismarck* or *Tirpitz* 42,000 tons, four gun turrets with 15-inch twin-barrels, five naval aircraft. Cleared for action. Putting out today. Probably invasion of Iceland.'

He sent out a lot more information. True and false. For many of his sub-agents, whom he trusted, were playing a double game. Arne sat at the tapper grim-faced. He had two children and a pretty young wife. He had a prosperous business. But he neglected everything. He had only one thought, one goal – and one hatred.

He would listen to the answer to his radio message with an ordinary wireless set in his main office. The room was far too hot, but Arne Svjenrod dared not open the windows.

Now, on the way to his office, his fate overtook him. Only a hundred yards away, the security forces had listened in to his message. It was immediately decoded, Commander Steinbrinck of the security forces nodded. 'Right,' he said. 'This is it.' Everything was ready. The security forces struck.

They caught Arne Svjenrod in the entrance hall, Two men in civilian clothes came towards him.

'Hands up,' they cried.

He hesitated and felt in his pocket, then there was a bang. He slumped forward. The first man to die in Operation *Bismarck* was a Norwegian.

Lieutenant-Commander Werner Nobis was preparing to go on watch. As soon as the *Bismarck* put out, he would take up his position in the chart-room and assist the First Navigation Officer. He was tall, broad-shouldered, young; he looked like a modern Viking who was fond of eating caviar and kissing women. He would preserve his trim appearance and air of relaxed self-assurance when all sorts of other values had gone by the board.

The Lieutenant-Commander was one of the few who were heading for the Atlantic without illusions. He knew war at sea. His Knight's Cross hung on his locker. He never wore it, either now or later, when the fighting was over. He had reached that point already. But he was to go a great deal further...

Nobis felt none of the patriotic fervour that possessed the others, nor did he face death with the same stolid unthinking acceptance as the mass of fighting-men.

He had been drawn to seafaring by something very different from the merciless war at sea. He donned the blue jacket as a lad of sixteen because of the breadth of the ocean, the play of wind and waves, the sun with its thousand twinkling lights and also from a desire for adventure.

He entered the merchant service, passed without incident through all its stages and difficulties, and went aboard the French luxury liner *Ile-de-France* as a 'Second Fourth Officer'. They liked to collect handsome young officers of various nationalities, whom they put on 'social watch'. Instead of taking reckonings he played deck tennis with the lonely wives of millionaires and stilled the hunger for life felt by dollar princesses.

There was never any question of service on the bridge...

A steward knocked on the cabin door of Mrs Webster, in whose husband's business a thousand head of cattle were slaughtered daily. Nobis freed himself from the middle-aged woman's embrace, by no means un-willingly, and took the telegram.

It was his call-up to the German Navy.

He said goodbye at Le Havre. He talked for the last time with his friends, who were now to be his enemies. He shook hands with tall young Olly, who resembled him like a brother. They slapped one another on the back, avoided each other's eyes and laughed at their suppressed sentimentality.

Olly also had his call-up in his pocket. To the Royal Navy...

The training period was over quickly. Six months later Nobis was already at sea again. He hunted British cargo boats, fired at British aircraft, took over prize ships, led convoys through the Channel, put mines out of action and laid mines, sank and was sunk.

Then Deina came along.

At the wrong place and at the wrong time.

As a Lieutenant commanding a tiny sloop he had chugged along the Spanish-Portuguese coast close to the three-mile limit. He was lying in wait for an Australian egg boat that was late. As a result he ran out of oil and water.

Taking matters into his own hands, Nobis got in touch with the neutral Portuguese. He hoisted the quarantine flag and ran into Oporto harbour. The Portuguese had promised to fill his tanks. They kept their promise. But now he was trapped and could move neither forward nor back. For tied up to the Oporto pier was a British corvette that had just completed repairs. Likewise by misusing the quarantine flag...

Nobis was the only one of his crew allowed ashore. He was given twenty-four hours, in addition to water and oil. Then he must put to sea. The British ship would lie in wait for him and sink him with her first salvo. Unless a miracle happened...

The young officer wandered dejectedly through the streets of the harbour, to which he had looked forward so eagerly during the last few hours. He ended up in a tavern where whores put out of work by the war lay in wait for him. He bought them a round of drinks and afterwards got rid of them. Then he drank his cares away, or as far away as his situation permitted.

The Portuguese were pro-German. As a special favour to him, the two-piece orchestra kept playing a German song over and over again. Heaven knows where they got the music from.

Nobis racked his brains for a way out, knowing there could be none. He was responsible for a boat and twenty-one men. Twenty-one fine lads who would follow him through thick and thin and who envied his leave. The Captain is the last to leave a sinking ship – but he is the first to go ashore.

Then the door opened.

At first he saw only her.

She was slim, tall and blonde. She was elegant and self-assured. She was so out of place in the tavern that she had no hesitation in entering it. Nobis forbade his eyes to stare at her, but his eyes acted on their own. Then he caught sight of the man. Only a fleeting glimpse, from the side. Not a Portuguese, Nobis noticed.

Then he stiffened.

It was Olly, his friend from the *Ile-de-France*, Olly the Englishman, who just like himself was wearing an ill-fitting navy-blue suit and bore such a ludicrous resemblance to him.

The same instant Olly recognized him too.

The friends hesitated for a second only, then they walked over to one another laughing. Crazy coincidence had brought them together.

Then they lapsed into an embarrassed silence. Olly raised his glass.

'It's a lousy business,' he said. 'Cheers. There's nothing for it. Tomorrow we must fire at one another, today we'll get drunk together.'

It was a good thing the Principal of his Staff College couldn't hear him.

'Your tub by the pier?' asked Nobis.

Olly nodded.

'Your nut-shell a bit farther along?'

It was Nobis's turn to nod.

They laughed, but they didn't feel like laughing. They understood their position. And they were friends, one of them German, the other British –

under orders to be enemies and obliged to show the reserve expected of naval officers.

Olly's companion was called Deina. Olly had been friendly with her father. Werner Nobis sat beside her. She wore a close-fitting dress that she had probably made herself. Nobis couldn't help looking at her all the time. She noticed, but was neither angry nor embarrassed. Once or twice he touched her as though by chance. The contact made him forget everything, but only for a matter of minutes that were already numbered.

They rose and left. Deina in the centre. It was only a few hundred yards to the harbour. A fresh breeze was blowing in from the sea, rocking the two naval vessels as they lay facing one another.

'That's the way it is,' remarked Olly.

'That's the way it is,' answered Werner.

'Were you really friends?' asked Deina.

'Yes,' they both replied at the same time.

'Then the solution is quite simple,' she went on. 'One of you sails south, the other north – and when you meet again the war will be over.'

'We can't do that,' objected Nobis.

'We can't do that,' answered Olly.

He shook Werner's hand and avoided his eyes.

'I'll take Deina home now.'

Nobis nodded.

'*Mach's gut,*' remarked the German.

'Mind how you go,' commented the Englishman.

The two friends did not turn round to look back at each other. They gritted their teeth and cursed the war. And yet they didn't find out what war really meant until the next day.

Lieutenant Nobis thought of Deina and of his ship. He had no idea of what was going to happen, no idea that he would bring his ship home safe and sound and still less could he imagine that he would see Deina again and love her and that the war would then drive him away from her...

Lieutenant-Commander Nobis sprang to his feet. Sub-Lieutenant Peters had entered. Standing a trifle too stiffly to attention he reported : 'The Commander wishes to see you, sir.'

'Where?'

'On the bridge, sir.'

And that moment the flagship *Bismarck* weighed anchor. Nobis automatically looked at his wrist-watch: 5.02 p.m. The *Bismarck* was steaming out to meet the enemy.

She was going to the German Navy's greatest victory.

She was going to the German Navy's bitterest defeat....

The *Bismarck* hauled slowly and imperturbably out of the Norwegian fjord past Bergen. Closely followed by the heavy cruiser *Prinz Eugen*, a 19,000-ton ship with a crew of 1,400, which .was also going to meet the enemy for the first time. Out at sea the squadron formed up. Two minesweepers led the van. Five destroyers protected the flanks and the rear.

On the *Bismarck*'s bridge stood Admiral Lütjens, a man whom no one had yet seen laugh. Course 260°. Sea 2 to 3. Wind force 4 to 5. Visibility 22 miles.

The evening brought hazy weather. After 4½ hours' sailing the group met a convoy of merchant ships. The Admiral demanded the distinguishing signal. The convoy replied correctly.

It was a German sham convoy of eleven ships, protected by a light cruiser and two destroyers. The group had only put out in order to camouflage Operation *Bismarck*. It received the order to proceed.

The vessels returned to their home ports.

The protecting vessels were now also dismissed. The flagship *Bismarck* and the heavy cruiser *Prinz Eugen* changed course. When Captain Lindemann learnt what the new course was, he shook his head. The Supreme Naval Command had suggested that the group should break through to the Atlantic between Iceland and the Faroes. But, as Fleet Commander, Admiral Lütjens had complete freedom of action. Why he decided in favour of the far more dangerous Denmark Strait was something the German Naval Command never understood.

The order to stand down was cancelled. The crew on the upper deck kept their life-jackets and their steel helmets always within reach. From bow to stem, from keel to masthead, the ship was full of tension. All of a sudden everyone felt the ship's vibration, told himself it was quite natural and yet felt frightened – the young sailors on their first voyage just the same as the experienced officers, who wouldn't have shown their feelings for anything in the world. Each one reacted in his own way. Some talked twice as much as usual and others no longer spoke at all, some whispered, others shouted, some spent all their time in the latrine, others stopped going altogether.

Petty Officer Mehring forgot his stories about women. Link thought of his fiancee. Sub-Lieutenant Peters told jokes. But they fell flat. Those who spoke softly were shouted at for talking so loud.

Suddenly everyone felt the presence of the enemy, who might attack out of the night, out of the mist, from the air or from under the water. The fact that nothing happened for hours merely increased the tension. The men on lookout fought with spectres of the night. They kept seeing submarines everywhere. The grinning Fata Morgana issued one false command after another. They were cancelled, reissued and cancelled again. Nothing causes more turmoil than inaction when going to meet the enemy.... Sub-Lieutenant Peters had no appetite. But he made a great effort to disguise the fact. What the hell did I want to join the Navy for?, he asked himself grimly. He threw away his napkin and reported back to the chart-room. Lieutenant-Commander Nobis greeted him with: 'You look pale, Peters.' 'I'm always pale, sir... even as a child.' The same instant he turned red.

"You're not pale now,' commented Nobis with a grin.

'I'm not scared, sir.'

The officer slapped him on the back.

'No one said you were. Man, you've no idea how I felt the first time out. Don't tell anyone else, but I was sick twice a day.'

Now Peters grinned.

'Do you understand what the Admiral's up to?'

'No. And I don't intend to try.'

'The Old Man would much rather have sailed through the Faroes.'

'So would I,' growled Nobis.

He bent over the charts and put away the compasses.

'Lütjens probably thinks the British imagine we're taking the other route this time. The Admiral thinks round two comers. That's why he's an admiral.... If the British also think round two comers everything will be all right... Now I'm going to hit the hay for half an hour.'

Nobis left the chart-room, reported off at the bridge, took a few breaths of fresh air and crossed the alley to the shelter-deck.

At that moment Able Seaman Pfeiffer emerged from the officers' lavatory. In the confusion induced by being 'at the front' he had mixed up the 'heads'.

'Where do you think you're coming from?' Nobis asked him.

'Aye-aye, sir.'

'What do you mean, aye-aye?' Nobis laughed. 'Next time kindly check your destination.'

'Aye-aye, sir.'

The AB stood where he was irresolutely.

'Have you the slightest idea where you're supposed to go?'

'Not really, sir.'

'Which Division?'

'Second Seamen's.'

'Come with me.'

Nobis came out on the mess deck. The deck senior called out 'Attention!'

and saluted.

When Nobis stood among the lockers, when he smelt the fug, when he saw the pictures of half-naked girls – all at once he felt at home. All at once he forgot he was an officer. All at once he was there among the men who were sharing his destiny. The vibration disappeared. Not only for him, but for the others as well. For a few minutes. Only for a few minutes.

On the flap-shelf stood a half-empty bottle of brandy. A Leading Seaman was about to clear it away.

'Leave it,' said Nobis. He picked up a mug and filled it. 'Down the hatch,' he said. He drank the mug off at one draught. Then he stood up.

He suddenly remembered he was an officer on the *Bismarck*. And the ship was steaming on through the night. With 2,430 destinies on board that would be decided in a few days. By war, the father of all murder. With men on board who hoped, worried, trembled with fear or boasted courageously. Men filled with a sense o(duty, with anxiety, with trepidation. Towards one goal – destruction. Their own or the enemy's. Victory or death. But they had one aim above all others: to survive – if they possibly could.

What about the other side? What were the British doing? What did they think? What did they know? What had they to pit against the most modern of all German battleships? How many men, how much equipment, how many shells? How much courage, how much luck?

In the Admiralty the threads were running together. Threads that it was at first impossible to disentangle. The *Bismarck* was known as a miracle ship. Had she already put to sea? Or was it her sister vessel, the *Tirpitz*? What was her objective? Were all the reports from the secret agents in Norway correct?

The most important question for Admiral Sir John Tovey, however, was whether the German squadron had already left harbour.

Aerial reconnaissance alone could provide a certain answer.

That day, 21 May, 1941, the weather was so bad that the whole of the R.A.F. was grounded. Air operations were regarded as out of the question. After prolonged deliberation behind closed doors the British resolved to attempt the impossible. With volunteers.

...With Commander Rotherham, one of the most successful long-distance reconnaissance men.

Rotherham's experience seemed so valuable to the Admiralty that they had long since withdrawn him from the fighting front. Rotherham at once expressed his willingness to fly an old-fashioned seaplane to Bergen – at a height of 210 feet, in order to slip under the German radar net. His first objective was a small island 15 nautical miles from Bergen. From there the seaplane was to make its crucial flight over the fjord.

Without modern navigational instruments – it was normally used for meteorological work – the machine set off. It flew so low that the crew were afraid of being smashed against the cliffs of the Norwegian mainland.

Rotherham reached the island from which he was to take his bearings and flew straight on to the fjord.

He flew at low altitude through the blanket of cloud – and saw that the bay was empty. To be on the safe side he circled round a few times and then flew on to Bergen, to see what ships were in port.

Now the German flak began to rage round the enemy plane. Rotherham escaped in a power dive and radioed his sensational report to England :

'Enemy ships left port.'

The intrepid pilot ran to the telephone in his flying kit. The Admiralty were ready waiting. To make quite certain, they wished to speak to the officer before embarking on their counter-measures. Every extra hour the British units could be kept in port was invaluable, for it meant that their fuel would last an hour longer.

Later the Admiralty also learned from a Norwegian agent that the battleship had put out to sea. Where was it bound?

One thing was certain, the German squadron led by the battleship had a start of at least six hours.

Even before the Admiralty knew the German Navy's plans, they mobilized their forces.

The heavy cruisers *Suffolk* and *Norfolk* set out to reconnoitre the Denmark Strait.

The *Hood*, the largest warship in the world (except for the *Bismarck*), the *Prince of Wales* and six destroyers advanced into the region of the Hvalfjord.

The cruisers *Birmingham* and *Manchester* received orders to patrol the west coast of Iceland.

Off Western Scotland lay the cruiser *Arethusa* with five destroyers.

The hunt for the *Bismarck* was also joined by Admiral Sir John Tovey's flagship, *King George V*, escorted by the aircraft carrier *Victorious*, four cruisers and seven destroyers. Even that was not all.

Off the Butt of Lewis lay the *Repulse* with three destroyers.

Round the Faroes lurked five British cruisers.

The hunters were beginning to close in on the *Bismarck*. The operation covered an area of 1,000 square miles...

A ghostly calm lay over everything for twenty-six hours and thirty minutes. For twenty-six hours and thirty minutes the eyes of the men on board darted nervously about without reason. Then it seemed that the time had come. The first salvoes rang out...

Shortly before this first alarm Surgeon Lieutenant-Commander Thiele had noted that Able Seaman Heinz Burger was going to make an exceptionally good recovery from his appendectomy. He lay in a snow-white bed in the sick-bay, but he did not appreciate the fact. Between the anaesthetic and the first stage of convalescence the ship's regular vibration had no significance for him. He would leam to fear later.

Shortly before the first alarm Captain Lindemann had his first harsh argument with Admiral Lütjens. No one heard it, but everyone seemed to know what was going on between the Admiral and the Captain behind the steel walls of the conning position. How far the officers' views on tactical matters diverged became horrifyingly evident after the sinking of the *Hood*.... A drama of discipline. A victory of orders over common sense. It was now 7.10 p.m. The watch off had messed – plums and dumplings. In fifty minutes the watch would change.

The initial tension seemed to have eased. Most of the *Bismarck*'s crew had no idea where they were. Their engine-room remained the same. They had the same neighbour, the same superior. They carried out the same operations. To their surprise and delight the more placid among the young sailors discovered how monotonous a voyage into action was.

Others reacted differently. A few men of the Third Half-Division of Seamen tested their life-jackets to make sure they were water-tight. One man heaved 17 pints of water aboard in a bucket and held his hand in the cold water to sec how soon it went numb. Everyone laughed at him. Outside the temperature was 10 deg F.

Lieutenant-Commander Nobis had just entered this temperature in his rough log. Then he had another hour off watch. The best thing to do with these sixty minutes, he had learnt, was to hit the hay. He retired into his cabin.

The four bare wooden walls, as thin as paper and modestly covering the steel beneath, suddenly gave him the feeling of being at home. Ridiculous! At home on a battleship! But where was Lieutenant-Commander Nobis at home?

All of a sudden he remembered Deina, with whom he might have been at this moment. In Portugal. In a neutral country. In the midst of peace. Miles are no obstacle to thought. Werner Nobis travelled away for ten minutes into memory. He took out letters and photographs. He forgot where he was, where he had to be.

That day in Oporto harbour, after he had said goodbye to his English friend, Olly, without turning round to look at him again, life went on. A life he wished to the devil, because it left him no way out. But which, thank God, the devil had not yet taken.

It was 1940 and the war at sea was still quite jolly, apart from the situation of the German sloop G 69, for which a British corvette was lying in wait just out-side the Portuguese three-mile limit. The then Lieutenant Werner Nobis had to go ashore once more to thank the harbourmaster for his help.

They kept him waiting. They had their reasons for doing so. They didn't want any warlike incidents off their neutral shores. A signature was missing that he needed in order to leave port. It was missing for several hours.

'There's no pilot free at the moment,' Lieutenant Nobis was told.

'How long is a moment?'

'Two hours perhaps.'

Nobis wandered ill-humoured and aimless through the streets of the port. In mufti, of course. As prescribed by the regulations of a neutral power. The night had given him an opportunity of getting used to the idea that he would be shot to pieces by his own friend Olly. Because he was an Englishman. But it would have been just the same if the situation had been reversed.

Suddenly she was standing in front of him. Concern for his men had long ago driven her out of his thoughts. Once again she looked fresh, young and elegant – Deina.

She laughed at him. He looked at her eyes and thought of his worries.

'Why arc you staring at me like that?' she asked.

'Is there a law against it?'

'No.'

Werner Nobis went with Deina into a cafe, ordered, asked her pardon and telephoned the pilot office. Of course no pilot was free yet. He had to wait and wait and wait. And keep his nerve. And sit next to Deina.

'What are you doing in Portugal?' he asked her.

'I'm living,' she replied.

'How did you get to know Olly?'

'His father was a friend of my father's. They were both sailors. They died a few years ago. Almost at the same time. I'm British,' she added abruptly.

'I'm sorry,' replied Nobis.

'Why?'

He didn't answer.

'I know exactly what you mean,' she continued. 'I grew up in England. My mother is Portuguese. When my father died I came back to this country.

I love it. And I learnt that you can prize two countries, even when they are hostile to one another. Can you understand that?'

'Yes.'

'I'm a bad Englishwoman. I should have been a bad Portuguese too. Or a bad German. England is no more to me than a land I respect. I have a British passport. But that makes no odds. Passports are a formality, it's people that matter, not papers.'

Deina was pink in the face. Her eyes were flashing. She spoke rapidly and vehemently. She took no notice of the people staring across at their table. Deina never took any notice of what people thought.

Nobis was gazing at her. He watched her eyes without hearing her words. She was aware of this, but disregarded it.

'Do you enjoy the war?'

'Of course not,' he replied.

'Look,' she went on, 'we two could be playing tennis now or going for a swim. Or we might have just met at a dance, or be keeping a date at the theatre. Doesn't that make you angry?'

'You talk as though I was personally responsible for the war.'

He got up and rang the pilot office again. He knew in advance that the answer would be no. But he just wanted to make sure.

'In an hour,' they told him.

An hour has sixty minutes. A minute has sixty seconds. And a second is not so short as a heartbeat. A heart beats faster when you are sitting beside Deina. They stood up and walked out side by side. At the wrong time and the wrong place. Side by side as though they belonged to one another. But they belonged to the war.

Both of them were thinking this, but Deina put it into words.

'What's going to happen to you now? Isn't it crazy, what you and Olly are going to do to one another? What you believe to be your duty. A filthy sort of duty. Your duty is to live, to marry, to produce children and rap them across the knuckles if ever they start playing with a toy gun.'

'I shall do that when the time comes.'

Deina smiled at Nobis, For a moment she laid her hand on his arm. It was a natural, involuntary movement, but in this second Werner Nobis became truly aware of her and loved her. In this second he learnt who she really was and that her picture would go with him everywhere. On long, grinding patrols, in cold and eerie nights, in the hail of shells and in the dreary tedium of home defence. Through the whole war, through the darkness of night, through fear, through horror.

A quarter of an hour later they faced one another for the last time. At least, they thought so. And the circumstances gave them every reason for thinking so.

Deina looked at Werner Nobis and smiled. Her smile was painful. He noticed it and for the fraction of a second he was glad.

'Now I must say goodbye,' he began.

'Yes,' she answered softly.

He wanted to tell her everything, but he couldn't utter a word.

'I shan't read the papers tomorrow.'

She turned round to him once again, then hurried away. People walking past in the opposite direction noticed she was crying. From now on things moved fast. Nobis returned to his sloop. As far as the three-mile limit everything was plain sailing. But there Olly would be waiting for him, with guns that wouldn't give him a chance. He would grit his teeth and shout the ranges to his crew. War's war! To hell with it all! If Olly thought things out properly he would expect Werner Nobis to slip away northwards. So he must run south. But what was the use of that? The British corvette was faster than the wretched sloop.

Nobis ran south – and the Australian egg boat he had been waiting for came to meet him. He nabbed her. At least he and his crew had a good meal of poached eggs.

The corvette did not show up; Minutes, hours, days passed. The sloop had long since set out on its homeward voyage with the captured 15,000-tonner under escort. Still no trace of Olly.

Olly, it turned out later, had worries of his own. The German security forces had a post at Oporto too. They reported the corvette's arrival to Spain. From Spain the report was passed on to the South of France. In the South of France German bombers went up to deal with the ship.

The first bombs fell wide. The second lot were right on target. The ship caught fire. The crew put it out. Half the crew that is – the other half had perished.

Nothing new in naval warfare. Who cared about the Ollys? The Ollys on the other side?

Nobis ran into Bordeaux harbour with ten million captured eggs. He was decorated and sent straight back into action. Later he learnt that Olly had escaped with his life. A fortnight later Nobis, too, learnt what bombs tasted like. What it meant to drift helplessly among mountainous waves and gaze despairingly at an endless horizon.

The war at sea had him fast in its merciless clutches. Nobis had a chance of breaking free. He met Deina again. He loved the girl and threw away his chance. He thought it was his duty. To hell with duty...

A signal interrupted the recollections of Lieutenant Werner Nobis, who had meanwhile been promoted to Lieutenant-Commander.

Air raid warning on the *Bismarck*!

'All hands to action stations!'

'Clear the decks for action!'

Then the gun turrets were already spitting out their shells...

Carrying out her orders, the British cruiser *Suffolk* had been searching the seas in this area. She possessed modern radar equipment. Before she located the *Bismarck* there were two false alarms. The first time it was pack ice, the second it was the *Norfolk*, the leading ship of the squadron. Both the pack ice and the *Norfolk* were at first taken for the *Bismarck* and reported to the Admiralty in London. At this point chance took a decisive hand in the matter. As a result of the mistaken belief that the *Bismarck* had been located, the *Hood* under Vice-Admiral Lancelot Holland, and the *Prince of Wales*, which had meanwhile put to sea with six destroyers, altered course.

By chance in the right direction.

For now the *Bismarck* appeared on the *Suffolk*'s radar screen. A new radio message went out.

The *Norfolk*, too, suddenly came upon the enemy as she emerged from a fogbank. The attempt to withdraw from the *Bismarck*, which was only six sea miles way, succeeded. The cruiser slipped quickly into the protection of the mist. Nevertheless the lookout on the *Bismarck* had spotted her.

Forty seconds later the first salvo ripped into the sea around the British cruiser. Shell splinters fell on deck. The German flagship was shooting true. The *Norfolk* doubled back and plunged 'full speed ahead' into the fogbank.

In the *Bismarck*'s engine-room the shots had been heard as dull booms. The men stood at their posts with pale sweaty faces.

'Was that our guns firing, or shells hitting us?' asked Link.

'Our guns, of course,' replied Petty Officer Lindenberg.

'How can you tell?'

'You can't tell. You've just got to be optimistic. That's all.'

Link gestured vaguely and aimlessly.

'So down here we shouldn't even notice if our ship was shot to pieces?'

'You'd notice all right, when you went up into the air. But by the time you'd notice it would all be over.'

'We're like rats in a trap here,' burst out Link. 'If there's a direct hit on the engine-room... If they flood it, we shall drown like rats.'

'Shut your trap,' exclaimed Chief Petty Officer Nagel. 'Stop driving everybody scatty. Anyhow the firing's stopped. And did you ever hear of a commanding officer flooding the engine-room of all places? You cowardly bastard!'

For the men the duel in the mist was over. How it would continue was known to a handful of officers on the conning-bridge, and to the *Bismarck*'s radar screen, that was locating the enemy in the mist.

The *Bismarck* tried to shake him off, but succeeded only temporarily. Again and again the radar revealed the proximity of an enemy vessel. The German flagship had no reason to fear the foe. What she feared were the reinforcements he would inevitably call up.

For hours the ships kept watch on one another. The *Norfolk* fell back. The *Suffolk* also maintained a respectful distance, like a small dog that sniffs at the heels of a large animal but dare not assail it. But the *Bismarck* had been identified and was now shadowed all the time.

The battle in the North Atlantic had begun...

On 24 May 1941 at 5.05 a.m., after being at sea for 36 hours and 5 minutes, the *Bismarck* and the *Prinz Eugen* came, at 60-5° north, 38° west, upon a powerful enemy squadron. The lookout reported:

'Battle-cruiser, about 45,000 tons. Four gun turrets with two barrels each, calibre 15 inches.'

No doubt about it, that must be the *Hood*. With a crew of over 1,400. With radar scanners. With pom-pom guns. With armour plating over a foot thick.

The escort vessel was identified by the *Bismarck* as the *King George V*. This turned out later to be an error. It was really the *Prince of Wales*, a sister ship to the *King George V*.

The two squadrons allowed themselves a bare half hour to form up for battle. The *Hood* was larger, the *Bismarck* more modern. They had now come to within about twenty sea miles of one another – within sighting-distance.

'Clear the decks for action!' came the order on both sides. Once in German, once in English. On both sides were men who had wives, children and mothers. Men who in the ordinary way were book-keepers, artisans, land-workers. And whom war had placed on the steel colossus. Of whom one group would conquer and the other die. As war decided.

Captain Lindemann turned to his helmsman and passed on in an undertone the instructions he received from Admiral Lütjens. He was calm, cool and collected. His face, so familiar to the crew, wore a frozen smile that did not leave it for an instant during the engagement with the *Hood*. What force of character and contempt for death this man had were to show a bare three days later.

He stood on the quarter-deck clinging to the rail with the strength of a bear. Two or three men of the crew, themselves marked down for death, sought to drag him into the water that offered a slight chance of safety. But he refused. For the first time in his life he shouted at his men. He refused to go with them. As he was bound to. A captain has to go down with his ship. Before this tradition the natural fear of death felt by Captain Lindemann, who in his spare time was a human being, capitulated. Suddenly all the man's impulses of self-preservation deserted in the face of his desperate courage.

He brought his right hand up to the peak of his cap and died like the hero of a second-rate film.

Only it wasn't a film, but a grandiose production directed by war, in which human beings were no more than extras.

But this time had not yet come.

For the moment death was at work on the other side.

Di-da, di-da, shrilled the strident alarm bells through the giant ship. The men rushed to their battle stations. Nerves vibrated to the rhythm of thousands of sea boots trampling across the iron deck-plates. The bulkheads slammed into their catches. Wasn't anyone going to stop that damned ringing? Di-da, di-da, it continued, as though it had not been heard endlessly protracted minutes ago (they were really seconds) by every man above deck, on the shelter-deck and the lower decks.

Clear for action, was reported from the gun turrets, the engine-room and the deck via the transmitting station to the nerve centre of the steel colossus, the conning-position. The First Officer reported to the Commander that the ship was clear for action, the report was passed on to the Admiral of the Fleet.

Hurried hands donned combat belts – gas masks, hammer and the life-jacket rolled up in the pouch.

The *Bismarck*, flagship of the fleet, was going into battle. On one side and somewhat in front was the heavy cruiser *Prinz Eugen*. This time it was a matter of life and death, victory or destruction.

The adversary behind the thin veil of mist was the *Hood*, the pride of the Royal Navy.

There, too, young men were waiting for the battle with fevered nerves, constricted throats and butterflies in the stomach. There, too, were only sons, the pride, hope and worry of their parents, men whom a war had taken to itself although they had done nothing to start it. A war in which their wives, their children, their future ceased to be of any account whatever. On both ships men told themselves with the same confidence that the *Bismarck* was unsinkable, that the *Hood* was unsinkable. And mingled with these interior dialogues was fear, denied by everyone, experienced by everyone.

To begin with, the two steel leviathans confronted one another from a distance of about 15 sea miles. At this distance they opened fire. In the course of the battle they reduced the space between them by 5 miles or so. The *Bismarck* was accompanied by the *Prinz Eugen*, the *Hood* by the new battleship *Prince of Wales*, wrongly thought on the German side to be her sister ship *King George V*. The cruisers *Norfolk* and *Suffolk* were also in sight.

It was 5.35 a.m. (Central European Time) and a few minutes later the most thrilling naval battle of World War II began in the Denmark Strait at 60-5° north, 38° west.

The *Hood* squadron was commanded by Vice-Admiral Lancelot E. Holland, an experienced officer with a high reputation, qualified by rank, long service and specialized knowledge. The *Hood* was a national symbol to the British. She was more than twenty years old and, when she was put into service, was regarded as a floating wonder of the world. She became the showpiece in naval reviews. Wherever the Empire was to be represented, the *Hood* made an appearance. Her picture was in school-books and hung in shop windows and on the walls of thousands of private houses. Although experts had spotted certain weaknesses soon after the launching, the public and the Royal Navy looked upon the *Hood* with reverence. But this exaggerated respect was to cost the lives of 1,416 sailors.

Admiral Lütjens drew closer and closer to the enemy squadron. He had to accept the battle that previously, in accordance with his orders, he had tried to avoid. The decreasing distance of the adversary was reported, to the German Fleet Commander more urgently every minute. Finally, at 5.52 a.m., came permission to fire.

The signal flags ran up to the *Bismarck*'s yardarm. The *Prinz Eugen* reacted immediately. Then the *Bismarck* also opened fire. The shells thundered from the barrels. In each of the four turrets stood sixty-four men. Sixty-four men with pale, sweaty faces, nickering eyes and dry, cracked lips. The huge, 15-inch guns were automatically loaded. The pause between each salvo was 22 seconds. The shells whined away in a south-easterly direction...

'Fire straddling,' shouted the First Gunnery Officer into the microphone.

The *Bismarck* was firing at the *Hood*. Her salvoes gained accuracy with every minute. Fountains of water as high as houses rose into the air closer and closer to the hull.

Vice-Admiral Holland made a crucial mistake. He confused the *Prinz Eugen*, at the head of the squadron, with the *Bismarck* and at first concentrated his fire upon the weaker vessel. His position was unfortunate. His ships were running towards the enemy exactly in line ahead, at an angle of almost 90°. Hence the *Hood* lay right in front of the *Prince of Wales*'s forward guns. Neither ship could use its aft turrets. They went into battle with half their fire-power.

But their fire was accurate. The third salvo straddled the enemy. Then the *Hood* received the first direct hit on her mainmast. From the *Prinz Eugen*. A blaze started and spread rapidly forward. The fire-fighting party raced across the deck under a hail of shells.

And still the *Hood* was firing at the wrong target....

On the *Prince of Wales* the damage was worse. She suffered hit after hit. A 15-inch shell smashed the bridge. It looked like a slaughter-house. Only Captain Leach and the Chief Yeoman of Signals escaped alive. Down the voice tube linking the bridge with the plotting-room a thick, viscous stream of blood poured on to the chart table. But right next door to it, in the gunnery control tower, the heavy blow was not even felt. The *Prince of Wales* continued firing...

Just as the ship's plane was about to be catapulted off to observe the target, the next salvo landed and damaged the plane. The wreckage was thrown overboard. What the hell's happened to the *Hood*? thought the *Prince of Wales*'s Commander. Why on earth doesn't she open fire on the *Bismarck*?

Now technical faults began to develop in the gun turrets. Barrels went temporarily out of action, the turrets jammed. It became evident that the ship had been sent into action prematurely, without sufficient trials. Skilled workmen from the gun factory were still on board. They took part in the battle in the gun turrets and helped to deal with the ever-renewed breakdowns.

The German flagship had also now received her first hits. Immediately afterwards the *Norfolk*, which was lurking in the background – she took no part in the battle herself – saw a plume of black smoke rising from the *Bismarck*. A shell destroyed the compressed-air control apparatus of the catapult.

At last the *Hood* swung round into a better fighting position. Too late.

The sea was ablaze. It was a hell of smoke, steel and flame. Destruction roared out of every gun barrel. The First Gunnery Officer, Commander Schneider, gave his orders coolly and calmly. They were firing slightly short. The next broadside, or at latest the one after that, was bound to catch the

Hood.

In the sick-bay lay Able Seaman Burger. Every time the guns fired he tried to jump out of bed, but Sick Berth Petty Officer Zeiger forced him back on to his pillow.

'What was that?' he asked. 'Our guns, or a shell hitting us?'

'Keep your trap shut,' replied the Sick Berth Petty Officer. 'You'll find out soon enough what's happening.'

Although the Able Seaman felt no pain, excitement made him hold both hands to the site of his operation.

Leading Seaman Link was thinking of his marriage by proxy and sweating. Lindenberg was shouting, although everyone could hear him perfectly well. In the locker the 'organized' brandy rocked to and fro. No one gave it a thought.

No one had the time or the peace of mind to think at all. Before their eyes, before their hands were the lever of the cold metal handle, the instrument board with the flickering signal lamps, and the loudspeaker with its everlasting announcements. None of those who carried out their manipulations by electric light below decks as though they were on a trial run, not engaged in a fight to the death with the largest battleship in the world, could see what was going on.

The next second it happened. The incredible, monstrous, unique event. The German Navy's greatest moment. The British Navy's bitterest defeat. The *Bismarck*'s stroke of luck, a stroke of luck that cost the lives of 1,416 men on the other side.

Another salvo thundered out of the guns. It must hit the *Hood*. The officers stared through their glasses transfixed. No explosion to be seen. What was wrong? Not one hit? Surely they couldn't all have been duds?

There!

A sheet of flame hundreds of yards high. A crash. It was all over in a flash. 42,500 tons of steel flew through the air. So fast the eye could scarcely follow. Molten metal hissed in the sea. Floating oil blazed. There was a cloud of smoke, fire and fragments of iron...

The *Hood* had blown up.

Not a sign of the crew. They were done for. Dead. Killed in a couple of seconds. Torn to pieces.

Swallowed up by war.

Only three out of 1,419 survived. As though by a miracle, for which there was no explanation. Midshipman W J Dundas, Ordinary Signalman A E Briggs and Able Seaman R E Tilburn were saved.

How did the disaster come about? A salvo from the *Bismarck* had struck the flood's Achilles' heel – the insufficiently armoured magazines. The shells pierced the steel plating and exploded in the magazines.

The *Prince of Wales*, already heavily damaged, watched the foundering of her flagship in horror. There was nothing left for her but flight, for the two German ships immediately changed target and were both firing at her. The *Prince of Wales* broke off the engagement. She put out a smoke-screen and did her best to get away. She hadn't much chance. The *Bismarck* was faster.

But the German Admiral reacted in an extraordinary way. He didn't pursue the *Prince of Wales*. This caused a strenuous argument with Captain Lindeman. In vain. The Admiral stuck to his incomprehensible decision.

The battle was over. The *Bismarck* had also been hit. And first of all they had to see whether the damage could be repaired with the means they had on board.

The German flagship was leaving a trail of ou behind her.

When the crew of the *Bismarck* learnt that the *Hood* had been destroyed, a wave of delight flooded the steel colossus and for a few hours broke down the normally strict discipline. Everyone was running about, shouting and yelling. Men embraced, roared themselves hoarse, punched one another in the ribs. Pfeiffer tore off his combat belt, threw it again and again on the deck and shouted:

'What a war, boys! What a war! What did I tell you? I knew from the start!'

'Take it easy, sailor,' a Petty Officer told him.

But Pfeiffer rushed on to the next group and repeated the performance.

Some were singing, others dancing. Enthusiasm knew no bounds. Pettinger turned somersaults on the deck. Maier II drummed with his fists on the bulkhead. Link tried four times to light a cigarette, but his hand was shaking so violently that the match kept going out.

Everybody told everybody else what had happened. The description went from mouth to mouth, growing more and more highly coloured, more and more dramatic – yet none of those who gave it had seen the sinking of the *Hood* with his own eyes. Only a handful of men had watched the *Hood* explode from the conning-bridge and the rangefinding posts. These few eye-witnesses – and a British camera that filmed those hellish seconds.

'Now for home,' cried Mehring. 'Home to mothers, children and all the rest. Newsreels, the gratitude of the Fatherland, flowers, girls, leave. Did you hear what I said, leave! In a week you'll see yourselves on the screen. Oh, you heroes!'

'No one's going to see you,' replied Hinrichs. 'And it's just as well. Otherwise the screen would tear.'

Which of those racing this way and that, yelling and roaring, thought of the men who had died on the *Hood*? Men who were also human, although they wore a different uniform, men who had the same worries, although they spoke a different. language. Worries about their mothers, their wives, their children. Which of the excited young men on the *Bismarck*, celebrating their victory with moist eyes, hoarse voices and unrestrained jubilation, stopped to think that tomorrow or perhaps the day after they would meet the same fate?

That they would face certain death not for two or three seconds, but perhaps for hours and days?

That they would die ten, twenty, a hundred times, wounded or maimed, floating helplessly in the sea, too tired to fight against the mountainous waves that swept over them...

On the bridge the victory was taken more calmly. At 6.32 a.m. Admiral Lütjens sent out the following radio message:

'Have sunk battle-cruiser, probably *Hood*. Another battleship. *King George V* or *Renown*, damaged and in retreat. Two heavy cruisers are shadowing us. Fleet Commander.'

At 7.05 a.m. Lütjens added a second message: 'Have sunk battleship at approximately 63° 12' N, 32° 00' W. Fleet Commander.'

A bare half hour later he reported the *Bismarck*'s condition to the Northern Command:

1. E engine-room IV out of action.
2. Port stoke-hold leaking, but can be held. Bows leaking severely.
3. Cannot make more than 18 knots.
4. Two enemy radar scanners observed.
5. Intend to run into St Nazaire. No loss of men.
Fleet Commander.

The intoxication of victory was followed by a sobering down. The war at sea continued. Since nobody knew how Operation *Bismarck* would go on from here, the 'wire' began to buzz again. Members of the crew whispered to one another that there had been serious arguments between Admiral Lütjens and Captain Lindemann. That was true. The two officers were not agreed in their assessment of the situation. This contributed substantially to the *Bismarck*'s undoing...

Thirty-two hours after the sinking of the *Hood* an invited audience of war wounded. Red Cross nurses, arms workers and people in some way connected with the 'Request Concert', a programme heard by an unprecedented number of listeners, assembled in the great hall of the Deutschlandsender in Berlin. Everyone recognized the voice of Heinz

Goedecke when he said:

'We shall now play for the garrison of pill-box Dora 23 in France *Woven kann der Landser denn schon traumen?*' Tumultuous applause. It was heard in Italy, Paris, Galicia, Czecho-Slovakia, Norway, Denmark. The broadcast, as usual, went off without a hitch. But the announcer concluded with a very special announcement.

He cried into the microphone:

'Now we have a request, a very special request. A request from the whole German nation for the gallant crew of the Battleship *Bismarck*. The song *Komm zurück*, "Come back".' At this moment the *Bismarck* was sailing along at the 'stand down'. The radio was on. On the mess decks, in the officers' cabins, even in the engine-rooms, the tune blared forth from the loudspeakers.

Lieutenant-Commander Werner Nobis had come off duty five minutes earlier. He might be recalled at any moment. But every moment had to be used to rest. He was too tired to sleep. He listened to the Request Concert between waking and dreaming. At the *Bismarck* announcement he sprang up as though electrified. He was not the only one. Suddenly, on the whole ship the jokes and the boasts were silenced. Irritation abated, recklessness dwindled. All of a sudden everyone felt that the message was addressed to him personally, that he was being spoken to from home, thought of his mother, his sweetheart, his father, and took out photographs and letters. Lieutenant-Commander Nobis as much as Able Seaman Pfeiffer. Some of them shamefacedly, others without caring about the comrades who were standing round them. Somehow the song touched them all profoundly. Yet none of them knew what a tragic significance this tune 'Come back', would acquire for the *Bismarck*.

In a matter of days. When the end had come. When shells were bursting and the masts had been blown away. When every nook and cranny was ablaze, a record kept sounding again and again over the loudspeaker, as though played by a ghostly hand, 'Come back, I am waiting for you, I am waiting for you.'

But by then there was no prospect of returning, only of dying...

The young Lieutenant-Commander's thoughts went back, over what seemed like an endless span of time, back to Portugal, back to Deina, back to the day on which he put out from Bordeaux harbour with his tiny sloop for the second time.

For the first two days everything went smoothly. The sea was calm and deliciously blue. Nobis sailed along close to the shore. On the third day came the first aircraft warning. A single British plane flew low over the boat a few times and raked her with machine-gun fire. A petty officer was shot in the stomach and died five hours later.

Several members of the crew were seeing a dead man for the first time in their lives. They watched in horror as the petty officer was sewn up in his hammock. With the German flag. There were always enough German flags on board.

Then Nobis sighted a merchant ship. He pursued and fired on her. But she escaped by zig-zagging. Her engines were more powerful.

The sloop *G 69* disappeared for ever.

A flight of four planes attacked with bombs. The very first fell close to. The second wave struck the sloop amidships. It broke in two pieces. Half the crew were killed by the bombs. Almost all the survivors were wounded. There was no need for the commander, Werner Nobis, to give the order to abandon ship.

Nobis was floating in the water alongside a few of his shipmates, but the current soon carried them apart. Then the British came back with their machine-guns. The bullets hissed close by Nobis. It looked as though some child was playing ducks and drakes with flat stones on the water. But they were not stones and they were not thrown by children.

Finally the planes disappeared. I've just got to keep above water, thought Nobis grimly. The life-jacket did this automatically. But he had to hold his head well up, for at this period the jackets were still of faulty design. I mustn't pass out, the young officer told himself. He lost all count of time, then came exhaustion. The current was bound to carry him to the Portuguese mainland. His ship had gone down some 7 or 8 sea miles from the coast. He fought grimly. But the situation became more and more hopeless. He had already swallowed water several times. He was already being overcome by a drowsiness that made him forget his terror of dying. Then they hauled him out. A Portuguese ship. Fishermen. They heaved him up. He was too weak to help. They laid him down alongside their catch and gave him brandy. He fell asleep from sheer exhaustion. When he recovered consciousness he was lying in a white bed in a hospital. A nurse in a dark uniform and a light apron was smiling at him. She said something to him, but he couldn't understand a word.

A shell splinter had wounded him on the left forearm. As though by a miracle he had not bled to death. The Portuguese gave him several days in which to regain his strength. Then a Portuguese naval officer appeared. He spoke English and was very polite.

'You've been lucky,' he said.

'Who else was saved?'

The officer shrugged his shoulders regretfully.

'Are you German?'

'Yes.'

'I'm afraid you are interned. But don't worry. You'll be all right with us.'

Nobis nodded.

'When you are well you will go into a camp... You know the regulations. But if you give your word not to escape, you will be allowed to move about freely. You've got time to think it over. I wish you a speedy recovery.'

Nobis grew accustomed to the strict nurse, the guards outside the door, the food, the smell of carbolic. His wound healed quickly. In a few days'he would be discharged.

He caught flies to drive away his boredom.

Then it happened. He didn't even look at the door when it opened.

All of a sudden Deina was standing in front of him. God knows how she learnt that he was lying wounded in a Portuguese hospital.

She was smiling. She looked fresh and pretty. As always. And she sat down on his bed as though it was the most natural thing in the world to meet the German naval officer here.

'You're getting on fine,' she said. 'The doctor told me.'

'Yes,' he replied.'

'Was it bad?'

'Depends on how you look at it.'

'For once this damned war has done some good,' Deina remarked. 'At last we are together.'

She kissed him.

'There's peace here,' she went on. 'Sunshine. And work for you.'

She smiled happily.

He looked at Deina and forgot everything. He gazed into her eyes and for the first time ceased to think of the eighteen men who had died on his ship.

'I've arranged everything,' said Deina. 'You need only sign some form or other and then you will be free.'

'Yes, Deina,' answered Nobis. He forced himself to smile. He knew he would not sign the form. But he could not and would not tell Deina. Not at this moment – this moment that had been given him by the sinking of his ship.

He felt her warmth, the pressure of her hands, her lips. He kissed her – and even as he did so, he was already thinking of how to escape, which he still regarded as his duty.

The duty of a German officer. A duty that had to be stronger than Deina.

All this was a bare six months ago... and now Lieutenant-Commander Nobis was on the *Bismarck* to fulfil this duty that had driven him away from Deina. He put her photographs and letters in his locker and threw himself on his bunk.

Just as he was falling asleep a seaman came to fetch him. The First Navigating Officer wanted to compare the dead reckonings of the *Hood* battle with him.

'The *Hood* has blown up,' Rear-Admiral Wake-Walker of the *Norfolk*, which was still shadowing the *Bismarck* at a respectful distance, reported laconically to the Admiralty in London. Winston Churchill had to pass on this terrible news to the House of Commons. It was a black day for Great Britain.

British prestige, even more than considerations of naval strategy, demanded that the *Bismarck* should be pursued, brought to battle and sunk.

What measures were taken by Sir John Tovey, the Commander-in-Chief, Home Fleet?

When he learnt of the tragic end of the *Hood* his squadron, headed by the flagship *King George V*, lay 550 miles away from the scene of the sinking. He was unaware that the *Bismarck* had been damaged, even though not seriously. His ignorance was due to an unfortunate coincidence. The Sunderland flying-boat Z/201, which circled over the *Bismarck* squadron shortly after the battle, radioed back:

'Losing oil.'

The station that picked up the message imagined that the Sunderland was losing oil and at first did not pass the report on to Admiral Tovey at all. Other attempts at aerial reconnaissance were frustrated by poor visibility.

Admiral Tovey lacked definite information. He had to reckon with three possibilities:

1. The *Bismarck* was making for the German supply ships already waiting in the Atlantic, in order to refuel and attack merchant shipping.
2. The *Bismarck* was damaged and compelled to run for the French coast.
3. The *Bismarck* was heading back into the Baltic to aid the propaganda campaign to boost morale by victory celebrations.

Sir John Tovey considered it certain that the *Bismarck* would try to break through the Atlantic to a port on the French coast and based his measures entirely on this assumption. The decision rested heavily upon him. It was to make history...

His main worry was shortage of oil. The Royal Navy had no supply ships. The 'fighting' units operated in such a manner that they could refuel at the numerous British bases. During an operation in the Atlantic, where there were no bases, lasting for days and involving frantic cruising this way and that, the ships were liable to run out of fuel. Moreover, the Admiral had to bear in mind the need for the Home Fleet to return to port after any fresh engagement with the *Bismarck*.

He assembled his units at 60° 20' north, 13° west. The *King George V* was joined by the battleship *Repulse* and the aircraft-carrier *Victorious*, whose air-crews had only just come aboard and had to take off from the carrier for action against the enemy without any preliminary practice.

There were also the cruisers *Galatea*, *Aurora*, *Kenya* and *Hermione*, and nine destroyers.

From the east the battleship *Rodney* was steaming to meet the Admiral accompanied by three destroyers.

From the south sped the battleship *Ramillies*.

Force H, the Mediterranean Fleet under Admiral Somerville, was on its way from Gibraltar. It comprised the battleship *Renown*, the aircraft-carrier *Ark Royal* and the heavy cruiser *Sheffield*.

The Fourth Destroyer Flotilla with the destroyers *Cossack*, *Maori*, *Zulu*, *Sikh* and *Piorun* lay in a Southern Irish port.

The destroyers *Tartar*, *Mashona* and *Somali* were patrolling for U-boats some 400 sea miles off the French coast.

The cruisers *Edinburgh* and *Dorsetshire* were recalled from Africa and barred the way southwards.

The destroyer *Jupiter* and the cruiser *Colombo* lay at 41° 30' north, 17° 10' west. Thus an area of 1,000 square sea miles was hermetically closed. Every available fighting ship was thrown in. Contrary to all the laws of tactics, aircraft-carriers sailed without escort vessels. Convoys had to relinquish their cruisers and destroyers for the hunting of the *Bismarck*. While Admiral Tovey set his fleet in motion for the pursuit and final battle, he received from the *Norfolk* the horrifying message:

'Contact lost. *Bismarck* and *Prinz Eugen* vanished.'

This meant that the German flagship had slipped through the cordon...

On this black Saturday, 24 May, 1941, the devil had the Royal Navy by the tail. First, at 5.56 a.m., its idol, the *Hood*, was blown to shreds of molten metal... then, after straining every nerve all day long to avoid just this news. Sir John Tovey received the message, 'Contact with *Bismarck* and *Prinz Eugen* lost.'

How could such a thing have happened? How could the German flotilla have vanished into thin air after every one of its movements had been observed, followed and reported for hours on end?

By midday there was nothing left of the silky blue sky. Snow squalls and showers of rain had swept it away. Thick, dirty-grey clouds came up, as though heaven was hiding its face from the merciless war at sea.

By this time the German Fleet Commander, Admiral Lütjens, had already made the wrong decision.

When the *Prince of Wales* broke off the action and the Fleet Commander watched the manoeuvre without a word and without reacting to it, Captain Lindemann turned to him:

'I suggest pursuit, sir. The enemy is on fire and cannot possibly escape.'

'No,' replied Admiral Lütjens coldly.

Once more the officers on the bridge watched an incident which proved that the two chief officers held totally divergent opinions.

Captain Lindemann went on;

'Then we should reverse course, sir, and put in for repairs, either at home or in one of the French ports,'

'No,' decided the Admiral for the second time. 'We shall hold our present course.'

There was no attempt at explanation. His gruff tone, his icy face and the tradition of unconditional obedience tolerated no contradiction – not even when the fate of thousands hung in the balance.

Hours later Lütjens still stuck to his decision.

He believed that the *Norfolk* and *Suffolk* were still shadowing him. He did not know that during bad weather British radar equipment of 1941 could not locate at a distance of more than 10 sea miles. The impulses from the scanners reached the enemy, but there was not enough power to bring them back to the starting point.

Lütjens gave the following message to the *Bismarck*'s consort, *Prinz Eugen*:

'Shall shake off shadowers. *Bismarck* will take south-westerly course. *Prinz Eugen* to hold present course for 3 hours, refuel from supply ships and continue war on merchantmen alone. Confirm orders.'

At 6.20 p.m. the *Bismarck* veered to a south-westerly course. The *Prinz Eugen* steamed straight ahead. From now on the two German ships operated independently.

But as far as the British cruisers were concerned they had vanished into the mist. Before turning away, the *Bismarck* fired a few salvoes at the *Suffolk* in the hope of getting rid of her for good.

The British did not know then that they would find the *Bismarck* once more – and lose her again.

Left to her own devices in the hostile Atlantic, the heavy cruiser *Prinz Eugen* ploughed her way through the sea without her flagship, the *Bismarck*. She would be brought to a halt by damage to her engines. She would repair her engines. She would reach the supply ships on her last drop of oil. With reduced power the *Prinz Eugen* would slip past the enemy units and reach Brest.

But first she lived through a terrible experience.

The date was now 27 May, 1941. At 2 p.m. spirits on the *Prinz Eugen* were down to zero. The *Bismarck* was no longer sending out radio messages. Enquiries from Western Naval Command remained unanswered.

The Atlantic stretched out before the *Prinz Eugen* in utter emptiness. It was then that her commander received the terrible news...

At this moment Able Seaman Heinz Tröger was working on a fog buoy. He was tall, powerful, pale, on edge. His hands were all thumbs as he worked. Behind him stood Petty Officer Döhring.

'You can go off watch, Tröger,' said the Petty Officer.

'No, sir, I don't want to. I... I can't go now.'

He suddenly flared up and yelled at the top of his voice.

'Let me stay here. I can't leave. I must stay here. I shall go crazy. I shall go crazy if I'm alone. I shall jump overboard or shoot myself. To hell with everything. I can't stand it any longer.'

His voice suddenly sank. He gasped out:

'I'm scared... I'm so scared I can't stick it any longer.'

'Pull yourself together, Tröger. I know it's a lousy business. Go and lie down.'

'I won't,' shouted Tröger.

'It's not over yet. Everything may be all right...

What do you think they can do to the *Bismarck*?'

Everybody knew the story of Able Seaman Heinz Tröger. And everybody knew Fritz Tröger. Two brothers, alike as two peas, only a year's difference in age, their father dead in World War I, they went to school together, attended the same dancing class, kissed the same girls, both volunteered for the Navy and both were posted to the same unit, exchanged leave passes, for hardly any of their superiors could tell one from the other, and spent wonderful leaves together.

Their mother fell ill. But she kept a tight hold on herself. When her two sons were home she made sure they didn't notice. Only when the time drew near for them to leave again did she give way, then she grew paler and paler, more and more peaky, stopped answering questions and asked none. She had brought the two of them up on a ridiculous pension, the gratitude of the Fatherland from World War I – her husband died at Verdun. His photograph still hung over the desk, and the flowers underneath it were changed every day.

And his sons grew up. She wanted them to be as strong, upright and able as their father had been, before a shell ripped his head off.

Then war came again, and the sons were taken away as their father had been twenty-five years before. They laughed as they said goodbye, though they didn't feel happy about it. But they were young and optimistic, and they were together.

Until a week ago. An hour before the *Bismarck* squadron put to sea the two brothers were called to the orderly room. They didn't feel happy about that. They had gone 'absent without leave' together. They had been in the *Bismarck*'s cells on bread and water together once already. Perhaps they were down for another spell in the calaboose.

The Lieutenant was perfectly friendly.

'Well, you two,' he asked, 'have you been up to mischief again?'

'No, sir,' they both answered simultaneously.

'We can't keep you together any longer.' The officer was striding up and down the orderly room. 'I'm sorry. After all, my brother is also in another unit.'

Fritz Tröger sprang to attention and blurted out through clenched teeth:

'Is there a regulation forbidding two brothers to be in the same unit?'

'Yes, there is. And here's your transfer. You can think yourself lucky, you're going on the *Bismarck*.'

Orders are orders. No argument. A quick goodbye. Before they knew what had happened. Operation 'Rhine Exercise' had started. Able Seaman Fritz Tröger was on board the *Bismarck* and Able Seaman Heinz Tröger on the *Prinz Eugen*, where a heart-rending announcement over the loudspeaker had just shattered the gloomy silence.

It was heard simultaneously all over the ship. In the engine-rooms, the gunnery control towers, the forward gun-house, the transmitting stations, the messes, the dressing-stations, the galley, the mess decks, the officers' mess, the petty officers' quarters, the magazines, at the electricity control panels, fore and aft, in the upper works, below the water-line : *Bismarck* sunk.

Finished. Done for. Blown to pieces. Disintegrated. Sunk. After a death struggle that lasted for hours. After Unending agony. After an agonizing end.

Those who could still pray, prayed. Those who could still weep, wept. Those who could do neither sat in a corner and stared in front of them with minds a blank. During these terrible, sombre, brutal minutes they learned to hate war. War the murderer. Death for a puffed-up nonentity. For the hollow, empty phrases of those who generally manage to survive the holocaust...

The despairing, crazy scream of Able Seaman Tröger was understood even by those of his shipmates who did not hear it. The man who had lost his brother, who would have to face his mother if he, at least, returned home, was hammering with his fists against the steel walls, beating his knuckles bloody, striking out wildly in all directions. Some of his shipmates took hold of him and dragged and carried him to the sick-bay on the shelter-deck.

Morphia set him free from his thoughts for a few hours...

When he came to, the heavy cruiser had left the wreckage behind her and was homeward bound.

The *Bismarck*'s little sister succeeded in slipping out of the witches' cauldron...

On the morning of that same day Admiral Tovey with his squadron was 350 sea miles from the scene of the battle.

Tension was mounting on the British side. At the Admiralty the Naval Staff were anxiously awaiting answers to the crucial questions. Where is the *Bismarck*? What course is she steering? Will she double back into home waters, make for a French port or con-tinue operations in the Atlantic?

To none of these questions could Sir John Tovey give a certain answer. In the afternoon he split up his forces. If the *Bismarck*, as he anticipated, steered course 180° the aircraft-carrier *Victorious* and the four cruisers *Galatea*, *Aurora*, *Kenya* and *Hermione* would draw closer to her. The Admiral himself with his flagship *King George V*, the *Repulse* and a few destroyers was barring the southern passage. All other units remained at the positions previously ordered.

Vice-Admiral James Somerville was making all possible speed northwards from Gibraltar with Force H, to join up with the Home Fleet.

Where was the *Bismarck*?

Yes, where the hell was she?

Somewhere in the mist.

Again and again Sir John Tovey sent out aircraft on reconnaissance. One Catalina had to turn back soon with engine trouble. Other machines were in the air. Nothing on sight. Again and again the same report. The weather was in league with the *Bismarck* and if it went on like that the German flagship would escape for good:

More machines took off. Again they flew low over the sea that had been carefully mapped out in squares. And again they radioed back their lack of success.

Except tor a Catalina of the 240th Squadron. At 2.32 p.m. it spotted the German flagship. Until 4.40 p.m. its crew never lost sight of her.

The British were now on the alert.

The aircraft-carrier *Victorious* approached to within 150 miles. Contact was maintained. But how long could they continue to maintain it? What were they to do if the *Bismarck* turned off to the north-west during the night? If she escaped from her pursuers by means of her greater speed? Her speed must be reduced, said Sir John Tovey. They must try to score a hit. A hit from the air. The planes on the *Victorious* must go up. But the crews were not yet fully trained. Should he risk an attack in spite of this? He risked it.

Shortly before dusk nine Swordfish and two Fulmars took off. As they rose off the carrier's flight-deck a strong wind blew up. It brought fresh squalls of rain and low cloud.

At 11.30 p.m., double British Summer Time, the planes spotted a ship they took to be the *Bismarck*. To mask their approach the pilots flew their machines up above the clouds.

Then they dived through the overcast.

At the last moment they were struck with horror.

That couldn't be the *Bismarck*.

The *Modoc*, an American coastguard cutter, had inadvertently come under attack.

The *Norfolk* signalled unremittingly. Now the German flagship had also noticed the mistake and was preparing for an air attack. It was bound to come at any moment...

Shortly before the attack the men in the *Bismarck*'s engine-room had come off watch. There was stew. There was pea soup with visible bacon'and invisible bromide. There was the intoxication of victory. The *Hood* was topic number one.

For today it had taken the place of women.

While the young sailors ravenously swallowed their soup they thought of their ordeal by fire, their first great battle, the duel with the *Hood*, and the phases of the combat, which had gone like this:

At 5.35 a.m the order was given, 'All guns load!'

Then, 'Raise steam in all boilers! Full speed ahead!'

Whether from her own guns firing or from a hit – the hull trembled. What did things look like on deck? No one knew. Orders came calmly over the loudspeakers.

'Starboard one and three, port two and four, orders carried out.'

Then came the range reports from the rangefinder on the bridge.

From his deck the Chief Engineer directed this chaos of valves, instruments and engines. As the battle proceeded he coolly checked the high-pressure, super-heated steam, auxiliary steam, condenser, vaporizers, turbines, boilers, lubricating mechanism, bilge pumps and boiler feed water.

'Port engine is taking steam from midships, pressure report,' he said.

The men carried out his orders rapidly and deftly. How do things stand? they asked each other anxiously, despairingly, coolly, excitedly, full of fear and full of courage.

A hit was reported from the bows.

Again the voice came through the loudspeaker:

'Port boiler-room has sprung a leak. Boilers are not yet in danger.'

Damage Control parties went into action. One oil bunker had been hit. The ship was losing fuel.

'Compartment Three, close the bulkheads, clear the compartment.'

The crew of Compartment Three raced behind the saving bulkhead. Four hundred tons of water burst into the ship, and were then checked.

'Shall we disconnect the boiler?'

'Boiler to continue in operation,' ordered the Chief Engineer.

Suddenly it was all over. Pressure eased. Then came the intoxication of victory. Relief was expressed in a wild outburst of enthusiasm. One infected the other. It was only a few hours ago, but to the men who sat silently spooning up their stew it seemed as though several days lay between. Even before they had finished eating another alarm sounded.

'Clear the decks! All hands to action stations!'

They came in flying low. Flak poured from every gun barrel. The British planes launched their torpedoes, zoomed away and tore in again.

Again a machine hurtled towards them and shot its eel at them. Hell and damnation, why didn't the flak hit them? Were the fellows drunk? The first torpedo hissed past a hundred and fifty yards in front of the *Bismarck*'s bows. The second did the same. And the third. How many times were the blighters coming in? Were they crazy? Then, thank God, the attack eased off.

Strong nerves are a matter of luck. Werner Nobis had them. While the torpedoes were hissing past he grabbed hold of a young Lieutenant who had inflated his life-jacket.

'Hey, you,' he shouted. 'Have you gone mad? What the hell are you doing running around the deck with that thing on?'

The Lieutenant came to a shocked halt.

'It's regulations, sir.'

'Take the damn thing off.... What are the men going to think when they see you running around with that on?'

The *Bismarck* dodged, the torpedoes,

'Hard-a-starboard.'

Helmsman Hansen operated the press-buttons of the steering-gear with the unfailing certainty of a sleep-walker.

Again the report : 'Torpedo track.'

Again the *Bismarck* manoeuvred out of danger. From a fifth and then a sixth torpedo.

Suddenly another of the eels darted straight at the ship.

'That'll catch us amidships, Captain,' yelled Hansen.

A few seconds later a tremendous shudder ran through the hull of the giant vessel. A towering column of water rose at her side.

The nickel-chrome-steel armour held. Bosun Heiners was flung against a bulkhead. He died of internal injuries.

The first death on the *Bismarck*.

'A torpedo has struck us. No appreciable damage,' the Commander reported to the Admiral.

At last the flak fell silent. The British planes turned away. Back to the *Victorious*. The carrier's radio beacon had broken down. Captain Bovell had all the searchlights switched on. Hungry eyes tore gaping holes in the night. The order came through to switch the searchlights off because of the risk of U-boats.

'What about my aircraft?' asked the Captain.

He left the searchlights on. The order was repeated. To gain time the commanding officer sent out a lengthy Morse message. Orders are orders. Then came the sound of approaching aircraft. Two Fulmars were missing.

The all-clear sounded. Immediately afterwards darkness fell.

Nobis returned to his cabin. Peters had taken over from him. He was angry about his anger with the young Lieutenant. He picked up his last bottle of brandy but one. Drink is the lonely man's courage. And he was lonely. It served him right. The fate of Werner Nobis, the Lieutenant-Commander told himself, was his own doing. At least his presence here was not entirely the war's fault.

Nobis might have been with Deina now....

In Portugal the wounds of Werner Nobis, the interned commander of a

German sloop, healed very quickly. Far too quickly, as a matter of fact. Not until much later did he learn to appreciate what white sheets and the tender hand of a loving woman meant. Too late....

Deina came to stay with relations in Lisbon and visited Nobis every day. What the two had to say to one another they had said long ago. Now they looked into one another's eyes and felt the pressure of each other's hands.

They were so much in love they had no need to talk about it.

Until the time drew near for his discharge from hospital Nobis abandoned himself to his emotions – and Deina. Never mind what was coming afterwards. He didn't want to think about that. Who thinks about things of that sort when he is in love? And yet he knew exactly what was going to happen.

Every morning the newspapers came. The newspapers of a neutral country. They wrote of victories. German victories. And Werner Nobis imagined he had to be a part of this Germany that was forever victorious.

But every day Deina came....

'What's to become of us?' she asked one day.

'Whatever we make of ourselves,' replied Nobis.

'And what are we going to make of ourselves?'

He shrugged his shoulders.

'You're very talkative today,' she commented.

.He grunted.

'You'll be out of hospital in a week. I had a chat with the doctor today.'

'I could have been out last week already.'

'I suppose you're afraid of liberty?'

Werner Nobis tried to get out of it with a joke.

'We Germans fear nothing in the world but God.'

'You're terribly German sometimes,' complained Deina. She had grown serious.

Only now did it strike Nobis that he always had to talk to Deina in her mother tongue. In English. ...

They sat down on a bench.

This isn't the usual thing, thought Werner. This is quite different. Much more intense. How can I ever forget her? How can I ever get over the fact of having been together with her? How can I ever find the strength to run away from her?

But I must, he told himself the same instant. Even if she weeps. Even if it kills me. Even if the world falls in ruins. One day this damned war will be over. One day we shall be together again. Not merely for an hour on a bench in the grounds of a hospital. For ever.

'What are you thinking about?' she asked.

'About us,' he answered.

'What about us?'

'I think it's wonderful.'

"Then everything's fine.'

'Yes,' he replied.

'You don't look very happy about it.'

'You have to fight for happiness, no one will make you a present of it.'

'You've been fighting long enough,' she replied. 'Now you're going to stay with me.'

'Yes.' Even as he spoke he knew he was lying.

There was Deina. Tall, blonde, beautiful. A woman with bright eyes and dear aims, A woman who knew what she was saying. And of whom you went on dreaming, even when she was already yours. She was there. And there was nothing lovelier than her, nothing lovelier in the world of Lieutenant Werner Nobis, whose ship bad-gone to the bottom.

But beside her there was duty. The duty of a Lieutenant. There were duties always and everywhere. Duties choose their uniforms, but in whatever uniform they appear, they are always the same. They always give the same orders – patriotism and battle.

Nobis had less and less time in which to reach a decision. Either he gave his word not to escape and, apart from a few restrictions, he would be a free man – or he didn't give his word. Then he would be interned.

That was the first stage in the direction of escape.

Perhaps I shan't get out of the camp at all, thought Nobis. Perhaps there was really no chance, perhaps all his problems would be solved automatically, perhaps he could do his duty and still keep Deina.

He knew from the start what he was going to do.

But he dared not tell Deina....

He must decide today. Good God, how could he bear it? When Deina was away for only a few hours he already grew restless. Where could he find the courage to tell her that things were not going to go the way she had planned? He must tell her today.

Then she was standing in the doorway. She was smiling as she did every day. The policeman whose job it was to guard Nobis knew her. She always brought him cigarettes.

'By tomorrow it will be all fixed,' she greeted Werner. 'What's the matter with you? Are you in a bad mood?'

'No,' he said.

'Then what's wrong?'

'Deina, we must be terribly sensible.'

'That doesn't sound sensible at all.' She tried to smile. She didn't want to admit that she was suddenly afraid. Afraid for the man she loved.

'I don't know how to explain. It's dreadful. But you must understand, Deina. I'm a German officer. I have no choice.'

'So you want to go into the camp?'

'Yes.'

'That means you will try to escape at the first opportunity?'

Werner Nobis made no reply.

'Don't be a coward, admit it!'

Nobis nodded, without looking up.

'In other words I mean nothing to you. In other words you want to sacrifice our love in order to get back into this crazy war.'

'No, Deina. It's not like that at all. And one day the war will be over.'

'I'm not going to wait for that, my dear.'

She rose and picked up her handbag. Her eyes were blazing. Her hair had become slightly dishevelled. It suited her. In a flash she lost her calm, her smiling confidence, her natural poise. Her mother's temperament broke through.

'I'll give you until tomorrow to think it over,' she flared at him. 'Either you don't go into the camp...'

'Or?' asked Werner in a small voice.

'Or you will never see me again.'

She was far too agitated to cry.

'I'm a woman,' she went on, 'and a woman can never forgive a man for leaving her on account of some stupid nonsense. On account of this damned war. You'll see what it's like! Be sure of that. Then you'll think of me and be sorry.'

Suddenly her anger died away. Now she was only a young girl fighting back her tears.

'If you want to stay with me, write to me,' she said. 'Otherwise please don't.'

Before Werner Nobis could reply, she was gone....

He saw her once more, once only. In the middle of the night, for an hour or two of breathless delight followed by a few terrible minutes.

His name was called over the loudspeaker. He was wanted in the chart-room. Lieutenant-Commander Werner Nobis looked at the time. Peters must be dog-tired, it was high time he relieved him. Who wasn't dog-tired on this ship?

As Navigation Officer, Nobis understood the *Bismarck*'s position. Why don't we make a ran for it, he thought, that's our only chance.

Like this they're bound to get us.

The night was pitchy black. It was raining heavily. The sea was growing rougher. The *Bismarck* was still holding a southerly course. Still pursued, watched, hunted. No sleep for forty hours – benzedrine tablets took its place. Submarine warning. Zig-zag course. The distance increased. The enemy was still visible on the radar screen.

Because of her first-class radar apparatus the *Suffolk* always kept closest to the *Bismarck* and maintained contact.

Often it would be lost for a few minutes, only to be regained, lost, and then re-established.

On the British ship they grew accustomed to this. rhythm.

Suddenly it was missing, and Captain Ellis realized that the *Bismarck* had vanished again – perhaps for good.

That was what Captain Ellis feared when he made his report and that was what Sir John Tovey feared when he received it.

Was the Royal Navy's greatest chase to end in failure?

While the British despaired, Admiral Lütjens remained totally unaware of the opportunity that Fate was giving him for the second time. He stood on the conning-bridge. All round, the invisible enemy was gathering. When night raised her veil, when the cold grey morning broke, the *Bismarck* would be pincered between the Home Fleet on one side and the approaching Mediterranean Fleet on the other.

The enemy's superiority would be overwhelming.

That meant death....

Admiral Lütjens didn't see his chance. If he had gone full steam ahead on the opposite course he could have escaped, under cover of darkness and the weather. The *Bismarck* would have been saved and 2,402 sailors would have returned home. Their mothers, wives and sweethearts need not have wept.

But the German Admiral despaired too soon. He gave up. In this apparently hopeless situation his mind was befogged by dreams of a heroic end. He saw himself as a kind of naval Leonidas.

He cannot be altogether blamed for failing to see his chance. But the mistake he made the following day was unpardonable – he took all the heart out of his crew.

On the deck occupied by the Second Half-Division of Seamen topic number one had been resumed. The flood was beginning to grow boring. Women are never boring. There are not so many women in the whole world as exist in the imagination of sailors. And those there are, are neither so depraved nor so noble as they arc described. Wish-dreams took command of tongues. The fighting man can still talk, though in most directions he has little chance of making himself heard.

Leading Seaman Link's marriage by proxy – due in two days' time – was a topic that never wore out.

'If our Old Man comes up to scratch,' Laucha said to him, 'you'll be home for a scrag-end of your wedding night.'

'He needs it badly,' chimed in Moessmer.

They laughed – they didn't know that their time for laughing was almost at an end.

'You idiots,' yelled Link.

'Now he's getting narked again,' said Berber.

'Leave him alone, can't you,' interposed Petty Officer Lindenberg. 'Have you boozed away all the organized brandy?'

'Man proposes – but thirst disposes,' rejoined Lauchs. 'There's not a drop left.'

'This is a lousy bloody war,' complained Moessmer. 'We fight all day long and then there's nothing to drink.'

'How much fighting have you done? ...Except with your guts perhaps.'

'Pea soup is the poor man's piano,' answered Berber.

'So I've heard.'

In twenty minutes they had to go on watch. These twenty minutes they wanted to devote to the redheads, the blondes and the brunettes whose lifeless images hung on the lockers.

Then a voice came over the loudspeaker. Cold and loud. A voice that gained immediate attention.

'Fleet Commander speaking,' came the announcement. 'Men, we have won a magnificent victory. That this day almost coincided with my birthday was a happy chance. We have struck a blow against the enemy. We have destroyed Britain's largest battle-cruiser. We shall do the same with all the enemies of Great Germany.

'The foe is out for vengeance. We shall have to deal with an enemy ten or twenty times as strong as ourselves. We shall face him with the same courage as that with which we destroyed the *Hood*....

'Comrades, the fight for freedom confronting the people of Great Germany brooks no consideration for the fate of the individual. If we die we shall do so thinking of our homes, the German people and our Führer.

'We must die that Germany may live. At this hour we cannot think of our own fate. Whether we are killed is unimportant. The important thing is that we should sink one or two more enemy ships.'

The voice was still cold and unfeeling. It betrayed no trace of excitement. The young sailors listening at their battle stations, in their quarters, in the engine-room or the sick-bay stared at the loudspeaker in horror.

'At this moment there is only one watchword,' the Admiral continued. 'Victory or death.'

The voice broke off as abruptly as it had begun.

The announcement had stifled the conversation of the young sailors of the Second Half-Division of Seamen. For a few seconds they blinked. For a few seconds they stared past one another, looked at each other, looked away, thought of their homes, thought of tomorrow. For a few seconds fear took possession of them, wild, unrestrained fear. Everyone thought of himself and looked at his neighbour. Tongues were dry and foreheads wet with sweat.

Pfeiffer stood up and buckled on his combat belt.

'To hell with it all!' he said.

Nobody answered.

Sir John Tovey will never forget that hour. There was an acute shortage of oil. He had to send the *Repulse* back to refuel. Warships were withdrawn from convoys in order to take part in the pursuit of the *Bismarck*, And again and again he received the same message: we are running out of fuel...

Ever since the Admiral's address, the crew had hung their heads. Of a sudden the space on the ship was too confined, the temperature too high, the air too close. Of a sudden they listened to every sound again.

Below decks there was no day and night. Below decks the electric lights burnt perpetually. When there was a crash it was often impossible to tell whether it was their own guns firing or an enemy shell scoring a hit. They felt isolated. And suddenly they became aware that the enemy was watching them. They imagined they could hear him training his guns. They could see aircraft going up. They saw enemy submarines. Everyone listened to what his neighbour had to say. Perhaps a man was lucky and his neighbour was an optimist, then he was consoled with talk about home.

Every section of the ship put out rumours. Though nobody knew anything definite, everybody wanted to know something. The officers were besieged with questions. But they didn't know much more than the ratings. Only they were more optimistic and disseminated confidence, even when they felt very differently themselves.

That is called leadership....

Bauer II was the first to go off the deep end.

'Where the ruddy hell are we now?' he yelled in the engine-room.

'Shall I tell you, mate?' Pfeiffer snapped at him. 'In the Atlantic.'

'But something's got to happen.'

'Go topside and tell that to the Admiral.'

Engineer Petty Officer Hinrichs came into the engine-room. He was immediately assailed with questions.

'Take it easy, lads,' he said. 'After all, you're on a warship, not a pleasure steamer.'

'But what's going on?'

'Nothing's going on.'

'What enemy ships are near by?' asked Pfeiffer.

'Am I God Almighty?'

'But we must have some idea.'

'Perhaps the Old Man will let you look through the glass. Shall I call him?'

No one laughed. Jokes met with no response now. There was nothing left now of the famous *Bismarck* feeling, the conviction that nothing could happen to you on the *Bismarck*, that the builders had thought of everything. That enemy torpedoes would bounce off like snowballs. That hostile aircraft would be shot down before they could fire a shell. That the enemy ships were inferior...

The *Bismarck* had been hit. 'Damage negligible,' the ratings were told. But would the command admit it, if the damage was serious?

And what about the trail of oil? Why was their speed so low? The *Bismarck* was capable of another six knots. And how long would the oil last? What had happened to the supply ships? Perhaps the Tommies had put paid to them...

'I can't stand any more of it!' yelled Ebinger, the thin little AB who was normally tranquillity itself. 'I can't go on.'

'Go to hell! Hinrichs shouted at him.

'Leave him alone!' bellowed Pfeiffer aggressively. 'Otherwise you'll have me to deal with.'

'Fine shipmates you are.'

'Go back where you belong. We've enough trouble-makers without you.'

'I can't stand any more of it,' cried Ebinger for the second time in the background. His thin boyish face looked grey and old. He was at the end of his tether. He was seventeen years and four months old. Eight months in the navy. A volunteer. His parents' only son. Faithful till death, people said later...

But before death came, Ebinger suffered agonizing fear. Every hour, every minute, at every breath. He sat dull and apathetic in a corner, wondering how he could get away from this accursed ship.

In the midst of the battle Commander Junack set him to cleaning the railings in the engine-room, merely to keep him occupied, merely to stop him from infecting the rest with his terror.

The rest had better nerves. But they, too, became Ebingers when it was a matter of life and death. They, too, kept looking at their watches, counting the minutes to daybreak, listening to noises. Their eyes blinked too. Their lips, too, were cracked and their tongues dry.

An eerie feeling spread through the *Bismarck*, took possession of the crew and paralysed them. The feeling that the German flagship was sailing to a horrible end...

This day, 25 May, 1941, was filled with enormous, unbearable tension, though not a shot was fired. Fate played queer and deadly jokes on both sides, on the Germans as on the British.

First the *Bismarck* shook off her pursuers without knowing it. Then, again without knowing it, she gave herself away through a radio message. The British knew her position, but they calculated it incorrectly. For almost seven hours Sir John Tovey steamed in the wrong direction, thus giving the German flagship a start. Once more the *Bismarck* escaped, for the last time....

At 4 a.m. the officers on the bridge of *King George V* decided to wake Admiral Sir John Tovey, who was taking a few hours' rest.

Tovey was a small, relaxed officer who generally spread a wave of optimism around him. But there was not much sign of this as he stood in the chart-room – just twenty-four hours after the tragedy of the *Hood* – pondering the ghastly news, '*Bismarck* has vanished.'

In Sir John Tovey's view the German flagship had three possibilities:

1. She could make for a supply ship in the south.
2. She could run into a base on the Atlantic coast of France or possibly in West Africa.
3. She might return to Germany for repairs.

The Admiral could leave no possibility out of consideration. He was certain the *Bismarck* had been hit. But he also knew that any damage she had suffered was insufficient to cause any marked reduction in her operational efficiency. After the attack by torpedo-firing planes she was still doing a speed of more than 20 knots. What could the 18-inch aircraft torpedoes do to a battleship whose armour plating was designed to withstand the 21-inch torpedoes fired by submarines?

We must search for the German flagship in four directions, thought Sir John Tovey bitterly. We must be on the alert in the north-west, in the direction of Greenland, and we must keep the area round the Azores and Canary Islands in the south-west under observation. We must maintain a barricade from south-east to east-south-east to prevent a breakthrough to Brest, St Nazaire, Ferrol or Dakar. Finally there is the danger of the *Bismarck* returning to Germany via the north-east.

To deprive the vanished enemy of all these chances Sir John Tovey would have required the whole fleet of the Empire. He had to decide in favour of one course or the other. He chose to assume the alternative most dangerous to Britain – that the *Bismarck* would slip through the cordon and reach a supply ship lying somewhere between south, west and north-west.

Captain Ellis with the *Suffolk* raced westward and then continued on his previous course. The *Norfolk* held course 285°. Rear-Admiral Wake-Walker detailed the severely damaged *Prince of Wales* to Sir John Tovey's squadron. The north-western sector was controlled by the aircraft of *Victorious*.

In the early morning the *Repulse* sailed back to Newfoundland to refuel. The *Rodney* steamed south-west all night long at maximum speed. Because of heavy seas the destroyers *Somali*, *Mashona* and *Tartar* were unable to keep pace with the *Rodney* and were left behind. The *London* was set to watch for German tankers round about the Canary Isles. The *Ramillies* lay 400 sea miles south of the *Bismarck*'s last position. The cruiser *Edinburgh* lay 300 sea miles south-east of the *Ramillies*.

Force H – approaching from the south – was still some 1,300 sea miles from the area of operations.

All in all, the British position was desperate. Oil was running low. The ships had already received the order to cease running at 'full speed ahead', to save fuel. The hunt for the *Bismarck* could not be continued for very much longer. Another day or two and it would have to be abandoned.

Then a miracle happened. So unexpected and unlikely that at first the British could not believe it.

The *Bismarck* sent out a radio call.

This enabled the British to locate the German flagship and calculate her position...

Admiral Lütjens refused to go off duty. He stood on the Admiral's bridge of the *Bismarck*, exhausted, motionless.

He was standing on the spot at which he was to die.

But of this the German Admiral had no idea, otherwise he would have acted differently, otherwise he would have saved the *Bismarck* and brought 2,402 men safely home. He would have saved all of them except Bosun Heiners, who was flung against a bulkhead by the blast from a torpedo and fatally injured.

Admiral Lütjens imagined he was still being dogged by the enemy. This error led him to make his most serious mistake. In the early morning of 25 May he established radio contact with the German Western Naval Command. He gave himself away without realizing it. He radioed: 'Enemy radar apparatus with range of at least 35,000 yards is seriously hampering operations in Atlantic. Own ships located in Denmark Strait. Enemy is maintaining contact. Impossible to shake off enemy, in spite of very favourable weather conditions. Refuelling possible only if we succeed in shaking off enemy by superior speed... Own expenditure of ammunition in *Hood* battle, 93 rounds. *Prinz Eugen* managed to break away because *Bismarck* attacked cruisers and battleship in fog. Own radar breaking down frequently, especially while own guns are firing. Fleet Commander.'

At 8.46 a.m. of the same day the German Western Naval Command in France answered. Once again Lütjens had a tremendous opportunity to escape, for on land they had realized what Lütjens was unaware of – that the enemy had lost touch with the *Bismarck*. The radio message ran:

'Last report of contact 0213 hours from "K3G". Concluded with three-figure tactical signal, but no open statement of position. Impression here that con-tact has been lost. Operational radio signals to Bermudas and Halifax repeated, but not for Gibraltar or Force H, thought to be in Atlantic. Western Command.'

Nevertheless the Admiral held to his previous course.

The course that led to death....

The men had their tails between their legs. One infected the other. What ages it seemed since they set out on this sortie. How much longer would it last? Was there no end to this raging sea? What more could they do?

They wanted to go home, their duty fulfilled, the *Hood* destroyed. The *Bismarck* was in need of repairs. Nothing serious. After that another sortie. Of course. But no more this time. Now there was only one watch-word: set a course for home or France, and France, too, was home, so long as it was occupied.

Most of them left their food. It had no taste. And yet other forces envied the Navy its good food. Nothing was stinted. The meat floated in great lumps in the soup. But nobody felt like fishing them out. Nobody had any appetite. Everybody had a feeling of constriction in stomach and throat.

Lauchs entered in great excitement.

'Lads, everything's okay,' he shouted. 'In four hours we shall reach the coast.'

'What makes you think that?'

'Lindenberg told me.'

'How does Lindenberg know?'

'How should I know that?'

'If you don't know anything, keep your trap shut,' retorted Pfeiffer angrily. 'Before you turn the whole ship upside down with your latrine rumours.'

'Go to hell,' replied Lauchs savagely.

'Got the wind up, eh? And as soon as you're back home you'll start shooting your mouth again, no doubt.'

'Pipe down, or I'll knock your teeth in.'

The two men stood facing each other with their heads down. Exasperation spread over the ship. Every innocent exchange threatened to degenerate into violence. And yet they were all in the same boat, they all had the same feeling of drifting around the sea in an armoured tin-can, waiting – for the next attack, the next salvo of shells, the next torpedoes. Waiting at the mercy of this blasted duty they had to fulfil, of this murderous war at sea, of fear and horror, of endless, inescapable hours, waiting by some instrument, some lever, some press button, at their battle stations.

The 'blues' stalked through the ship. Today they had seized Pollack, the stocky Leading Seaman whom nothing upset. Today he was hopeless. He didn't answer when spoken to. He stared in front of him with a crazed expression. Suddenly he flared up.

'I can't stand it any more. The child must be there by now.'

'Take it easy, chum,' said Pfeiffer. 'You're not the one that's having it.'

'My wife,' groaned Pollack. 'It must have come yesterday... I'll go crazy if I don't hear soon.'

'Well, maybe they'll send you a services letter by helicopter. What a fuss you're kicking up. Having a baby is nothing to make a song and dance about.'

'Get on with your dinner,' Moessmer bawled at him.

'I can't.'

'Get on with your dinner, chum. First-class marching rations for a trip to heaven. You don't want to drown on an empty stomach, do you?'

'After eating sit and talk, or else go for a nice long walk,' remarked Lindenberg.

Pfeiffer put his 'mess-traps' away.

'We ought to have women on the old tub,' he said, 'then I'd like to see you. Then there'd be no complaints, eh? The Tommies could come as often as they liked and you wouldn't even notice.'

'The Eyeties have women on board,' commented someone.

'Nonsense... And if they have, they're only for the officers.'

'Oh well, when they've had enough, it'll be your turn.'

'For that he'd even take an officers' course,' com-mented Pfeiffer.

They laughed. For a few seconds topic number one made them forget they were on the *Bismarck*.

'My poor wife,' groaned Pollack.

'You silly mutt... Your wife's a lot better off than you are. You'll be washing nappies soon enough.'

The Senior Seaman stood up and buckled on his combat belt.

'Gentlemen, time to go on watch. You're a low-down lot. You've nothing else in your heads but food, women and leave.'

'That's something anyhow,' retorted Moessmer tardy. 'You haven't got a head at all, only a pumpkin.'

'And it's soft at that,' added Pfeiffer.

They left their deck unhurriedly. They had plenty of time. And time was torturing their nerves. This can undermine even a sailor....

It did indeed undermine them. Every hour, every 105 minute. When nothing happened, most happened. Because they didn't know what was happening.

The *Bismarck* was sending out a radio message. Incredible! But there could be no doubt about it. British radio-location was working at full pitch. How could such a thing have happened? But that was not Sir John Tovey's headache...

The Admiralty was following the course of Operation *Bismarck* intently. The radio-locations entered in the charts aboard *King George V*, the British flagship, were not all in agreement. Two pointed south past the *Bismarck*'s last position. But all the rest pointed northwards.

Sir John decided to ignore the southerly locations.

This placed the *Bismarck* at 57° north, 33° west. If this location was correct the *Bismarck* was heading back northward.

King George V immediately informed all other British warships. They were now to direct their operations towards what was calculated to be the *Bismarck*'s new position. They were not assigned to any fresh areas and until further notice could operate independently.

The *Suffolk* headed for Iceland. The *King George V* shaped a course for the North Sea. The *Prince of Wales*, already abreast of the British flagship, doubled back in the direction of the Denmark Strait. The *Victorious* steered for the Iceland-Faroes area. The *Rodney* hesitated. She was too far from the *Bismarck*'s estimated position. She was bound to arrive too late for a battle in the North Sea whatever happened.

The Admiralty studied the new situation. One of its most experienced tacticians, Captain Daniel, was asked to state his view of the position.

'It is my opinion,' he said, 'that the *Bismarck* is making for a French port. Whether she is seriously damaged, we do not know. We may confidently suppose at least one torpedo went home. On this assump-tion, her operational efficiency must at least be reduced. To break through between Scotland and the Denmark Strait would be too much of a risk for the enemy. He knows what forces we have at our disposal and he must realize that we shall blockade this area with every available ship. If the *Bismarck* approaches the French Atlantic ports, she will soon come within the range, and hence under the protection of the Luft-waffe. Moreover, U-boats will certainly be sent out to meet her.'

Captain Daniel held stubbornly to his view. But opinion at the Admiralty was divided. Nerves were on edge. Fatigue, setbacks and uncertainty had left their mark on the officers.

A second officer, Captain Edwards, took a similar view to that of Daniel.

Once more aerial reconnaissance had to be called in. Once more it had to bridge over these fearful, despairing hours of uncertainty. But the flying-boats' range of action was limited. Three Catalinas went up. It was 1.50 p.m. Whether they would be successful was extremely uncertain.

What was going to happen now? Were the calculations correct? Would they close with the enemy at last? Could they bring him to battle? Would they be able to avenge the *Hood*?

Sir John Tovey hoped so.

He had no idea yet that his units were steaming in the wrong direction. He did not know that a quite ludicrous arithmetical error was making naval history. That a faulty reckoning had once more given the *Bismarck* a start of almost seven hours.

This time the start must prove sufficient. And it would have done ... if Admiral Lütjens had known he had it!

Sub-Lieutenant Peters sat in his cabin writing. A letter to his mother, a letter that might never reach its destination. Peters was on edge. Twice, three times he began .to write and then threw the sheet away.

'Forget it,' Lieutenant-Commander Nobis told him. 'Lie down and relax. There's no point in writing anyhow... In two days we shall be home. You'll be made a Lieutenant and your mother can welcome you as a returning hero.'

'I wish I had your optimism, sir,' replied the Sub-Lieutenant. 'And your nerves too.'

'It's inborn,' answered Nobis. 'It's quite simple: one man has a goitre, another has flat feet – and I happen to have strong nerves.'

'I don't know how you do it, sir,' Peters continued. 'You look on top of the world and smell of *eau de Cologne*, as though you were going to a dance instead of into the chart-room. It almost gives me an inferiority complex.'

Nobis laughed.

'If it'll help you, Peters, I'll gladly lend you my *eau de Cologne*.'

'Don't you ever feel afraid, sir?'

'Of course. But you can get used to fear, as you can get used to cleaning your teeth twice a day or living on snake's meat.'

'How is it you never show any sign of being frightened?'

'Listen, Peters, the only thing I enjoy on this damned tub is the certainty that no one can see how I'm feeling.'

'Have you ever been sunk, sir?'

'Twice, my dear chap. The last time in a ridiculous little sloop.'

'How did you get off the ship?'

'Quite automatically, Peters. It all happens so quickly that afterwards you just don't know what happened. But don't worry, nobody will have to get off this ship.'

'Do you really believe that?'

'I've been telling myself so until I do believe it. And I shall go on believing it as long as I have to.... Well, now I'm going into the chart-room. Take your time about relieving me.'

That's a fine philosophy, thought Nobis. Here I stand, playing the hero and talking a lot of tripe, merely so as to forget my own thoughts. As though I could ever forget them. As though I could stop thinking' of Deina for a single hour. As though I had not relived our last meeting a hundred times...

Things had moved at lightning speed. Nobis was discharged from hospital and placed in an internment camp near Lisbon. To the left lived the British internees, to the right the Germans and Italians. Separated only by a rusty barbed-wire fence. Separated only by an invisible wall of so-called ideologies.

Separated only by war.

On both sides they played football, ate the same food, read the same newspapers. Only their comments on them were different.

The Camp Commandant, a tubby Major, was a gentleman.

'If you've any complaints, come to me,' he said in greeting. 'I can give you almost anything. Except freedom, of course. But that's your own fault. Though, mind you, I respect your decision. I should have done exactly the same in your place.'

'Thanks very much,' replied Nobis.

On both sides of the barbed wire fence they dreamt of escape. Guard-posts manned by expert marksmen blocked the path to liberty. They did not take their duties lightly and would shoot without hesitation. At night the grounds were lit by searchlights. There was only one possible means of escape : to saw through the iron bars on the first floor of the foremost building, jump down into the road in the full glare of the searchlights and then run, run, run, as fast as your legs would go.

Three inmates had tried it before Werner Nobis. Two got away, one was shot dead.

Assuming I get out of the searchlight beam without being hit, reflected Nobis, what then? Anyone can see I'm a foreigner. My Portuguese is hopeless. I haven't a penny in my pocket. I'm wearing something like a uniform. They're bound to catch me in a matter of hours, if nobody helps me. Who could help me?

Deina perhaps?

Nobis wrote to her. Merely that he would like to see her. The answer came by return of post. A few short lines Nobis would never forget.

'Werner,' she wrote, 'I love you. I love you terribly. I still hope you will decide for me and against the war. I should be happy if you did so. And I shall remain unhappy as long as you do not. It has never occurred to me that, according to my passport at least, I am British and that I love a man who should really be my enemy. Please forget, for your part, that you are a German officer. If you can't do that you will have to give me up. If you don't want to give me up, write and tell me so. I shall come and fetch you the same day.

Deina.'

He didn't write to her. He had now been interned for four weeks. Four weeks during which he thought day and night about escape.

Now the day had come. The iron bars were almost sawn through. They could be wrenched out by hand.

Then came the jump into the line of fire. Perhaps they would be asleep. He hoped they would be asleep.

They weren't asleep, but their aim was bad. Seven, eight times bullets whistled past his head. Then he was in darkness. He didn't rush wildly away. He stopped to take breath. His plan was to go first to Oporto.

To Deina.

He had a bad taste in his mouth when he thought about it. He intended to beg clothes and money from her. He hoped he would be able to talk her into it. If I wasn't a 'hero', thought Werner Nobis, I should be a scoundrel.

God knows how he covered the forty miles to Oporto. He smeared his drill clothes with dirt and disguised himself as a tramp. Every now and then he met policemen or soldiers. They took no notice of him. It was a particularly lovely day. The sun was shining as though to render peace more enticing. As though that was necessary! As though Werner Nobis didn't value, didn't desire peace! As though he was responsible for this damned war!

He got a lift from a lorry part of the way. The driver, a reckless young lad, who paid more attention to girls than to the road, spoke to him a few times. But Nobis couldn't understand what he was saying. He looked at his map. Another twenty miles. He hoped there were no road blocks. He hoped it wouldn't occur to the police that Deina would be his first port of call.

But beneath this radiant blue sky the police apparently had other things to think about than an escaped German internee. After all, he wasn't an enemy. Moreover, this rotten war was none of Portugal's business. Sugar was short, that was all, and it wasn't unbearable. How many people in Germany, Italy, Great Britain, Norway, Denmark and Poland would have willingly gone without sugar for the rest of their lives if only there was no war? When night fell he was in Oporto. Deina lived in a country house on the outskirts of the town. Nobis knew his way around Oporto well. At least on the street-plan, which he had got hold of in the internment camp.

What would she say when she suddenly saw him? How could he get to her without waking the whole house? How could he speak to her without coming into contact with her mother.

He had imagined everything would be much easier. His shadow flitted around Deina's house. It took him an age to muster up the necessary courage, to suppress his irresolution and prepare himself for the crucial discussion.

He wondered which was her room. She had described the house to him during her visits to the hospital. He knew her bedroom opened on to a small balcony. The house had two balconies.

Werner Nobis was lucky. He guessed the right one.

He threw stones at her window. It was a long time before the light went on. Then he saw her. She had pulled on a dressing-gown and looked sleepy. Her eyes had to accustom themselves to the darkness.

Werner Nobis stepped out of the shadows.

'It's me, Deina,' he called in an undertone.

Then she caught sight of him. He could see clearly that she was glad.

The worst is over, thought Nobis – but he knew very well that the worst was still to come.

The discussion with her.

The parting from her...

'I must talk to you,' he said. 'How can I come up to you?'

'I'll wake my mother.'

'No, please don't do that... I'm on the run.'

Deina understood at once. She nodded her head.

'I'll come straight down.'

Nobis stepped back into the shadows. He would have liked to switch off his thoughts, but they had long since made themselves independent. So had his feelings. So had his eyes.

Now she came towards him. She was smiling. She looked the same as ever. Marvellously beautiful.

In this second Nobis forgot everything.

The purpose of his escape, his urgency, the police, his lack of money, his need for clothing.

He stood in front of her, put his arms round her and pressed her to him.

She wept with joy...

The *Bismarck* steamed along with 2,402 destinies on board. Nothing happened. The calm before the storm. One part of this calm was Lieutenant-Commander Nobis, who sat in the chart-room thinking of Deina.

He wasn't the only one, everybody had some Deina or other of whom he couldn't help thinking. But only one of them had had the chance of staying with her. And he had decided in favour of the war.

The call-up had saved the rest from having to decide...

For seven hours chance had a field day. Among the British. For seven hours practically every available unit of the Royal Navy pursued the *Bismarck* towards the North Sea – and all the time the German flagship was making for the French coast.

At 3.30 p.m. Sir John Tovey received a new state-ment of the *Bismarck*'s estimated position: 50° 15' north, 32" west.

The Admiral stared at the report in dismay. He could hardly believe his eyes. If this position was correct, the *Bismarck* was not on her way to the North Sea, but heading for the Bay of Biscay.

How could the error possibly have arisen?

The answer proved simple, ridiculously simple. The graduation of the charts they had been using was inaccurate. The Admiralty should have spotted this. They should have drawn Sir John Tovey's attention to it. But, as usual, what should have been done did not become evident until it was all over.

At 4.30 Sir John Tovey radioed the Admiralty to ask whether they thought the *Bismarck* was shaping a course for the Faroes. He received no reply. Sir John now decided to take matters into his own hands. He abandoned the chase into the North Sea. He told his units that in his opinion the German flagship was making for France. He changed course.

He changed it an hour before the error was spotted at the Admiralty. Admiral Tovey saved one hour.

But was it already too late?

Sir John Tovey had no difficulty in calculating what the mistake had cost him. He was about a hundred sea miles away from the *Bismarck*. Her exact position was still unknown. That would take all night to establish. The Admiral had only one hope left – the planes of the *Ark Royal*, which was approaching the scene of action with Force H. They carried out reconnaissance over a wide area.

Once more the weather favoured the *Bismarck*. But in the end she was found.

On the 26th, at 10.30 a.m., a Catalina based on Northern Ireland located a battleship. Position 49° 33' north, 21° 50' west. Course 150°. Speed about 20 knots. The Catalina at once sent back a report. Every British radio transmitter passed it on. On every British ship they heard the news:

'*Bismarck* found again.'

Found again at last and for good. After 31½ hours.

To begin with there was some doubt as to whether the battleship sighted by the Catalina really was the *Bismarck*. Only half an hour later, around 11 a.m., a Swordfish from the *Ark Royal* identified the *Bismarck* as a cruiser.

More machines were sent up. They took off under almost impossible weather conditions. Mountainous waves flung the carrier's hull this way and that. It was the first time the Royal Navy had risked a take-off under such circumstances.

It was worthwhile. The planes returned with the news that the enemy vessel was no cruiser and must be the *Bismarck*.

Air-raid warning on the *Bismarck*.

'Flying boat of the Catalina type,' reported the man in the crow's-nest. 'Height 12,000 feet.'

The flying-boat kept out of firing range. Then the Swordfish zoomed by. Also out of firing range. The anti-aircraft guns were still silent.

For how much longer?

Fifteen machines took off for the decisive torpedo attack on the *Bismarck*. It was 2.50 p.m. The crews were told there was no other ship in the area of operations. This was an error. An error that was to cost the British very dear indeed.

It took about an hour for the planes to reach the *Bismarck*. The fifteen Swordfish flew steadily along. Through wind, squalls of rain and wretched visibility. The enemy had to be located by radar. The crews looked at their watches. Where the hell was the *Bismarck*? They could see nothing.

Then the radar screen reacted. A target.

The *Bismarck*.

Now came the most difficult part of the operation. First the planes had to be brought into position for attack. They had to be hoicked up into the clouds. Then assembled. Formed up in order of attack. Flown in at low altitude. Then the pilots had to discharge their torpedoes. And hoick their planes up again.

Who was for it this time? Whose name would be on the shell when the *Bismarck* loosed her flak at the enemy in the sky from a distance of three or four hundred yards?

There was no time for thought. The planes dived through the blanket of cloud. Straight at the target. The first formation was upon the enemy. At any moment the torpedoes would explode.

Of all British ships the *Sheffield* lay closest to the *Bismarck*. When the weather deteriorated still further, the cruiser received orders to take over frqm the planes that had been shadowing the enemy ship. This was at 1.30 p.m. Almost an hour and a half before the Swordfish took off. At the time the order was given the *Sheffield* was within sight of the *Ark Royal*. No one noticed as she turned away. No one guessed that the Swordfish, which were just being prepared for the attack on the *Bismarck*, would torpedo their own ship, the *Sheffield*...

Shortly before 4 p.m. the *Ark Royal*'s radio officer reported to Captain Maund:

'Sir, the *Sheffield* is in the immediate vicinity of the *Bismarck*.'

Maund realized at once what that meant.

'When did the message arrive?'

'At 2 p.m.'

'Why have I only just received it?'

'We had difficulty in decoding it.'

'You know what it means?'

'Yes, sir,' replied the radio officer.

'Radio an open message at once: "Look out for *Sheffield*."'

At the very moment when the warning came over the air the first torpedoes were already exploding...

Captain Larcom was on the *Sheffield*'s bridge. The approach of the Swordfish had just been reported to him.

He watched them through his glasses. He saw them rise into the clouds. What the hell were they doing up there?

Captain Larcom knew exactly what a torpedo attack looked like. He knew because his ship, the *Sheffield*, had served as a target for the raw young crews of the *Ark Royal*'s Swordfish during manoeuvres.

'They're attacking us,' he cried the next moment.

The first machine was already coming in at low altitude.

'Full speed ahead!' bellowed Larcom. He turned the ship away so violently that she heeled right over. He zig-zagged.

The water rose in tall columns. The torpedoes were armed with magnetic pistols, and exploded as soon as they came within the magnetic field of the target's steel hull.

A second torpedo came and another after that.

Each time it was nearer. The hissing, foaming track along the surface of the water. The malignant, deadly projectile. Fired by their own people – and they couldn't defend themselves...

Torpedoes were hissing towards them from all directions. The *Sheffield* dodged them by zig-zagging wildly. Damn it, can't they see we're not defending ourselves? thought Captain Larcom. Doesn't it strike them as odd that we're not using our AA guns?

Again a machine dived towards them. Again the torpedo sliced into the water and slashed a frothing passage through the churned-up sea.

The men on the upper deck choked back their fear and stared at the water. Don't they recognize us? they were all thinking. They have flown at us every day, every day we have served as a target for their blank torpedoes!

Are we now to die by our own torpedoes? Are we to be the helpless victims of our own planes – more helpless than if they had been the enemy?

The last formation was flying towards them. They were quite close now. Their torpedoes were bound to hit. Three at the same time. There was a chance of dodging one or two, but not a hope with three. Anyhow, not when they were as close as this.

The planes dived and flew in low.

Now they must drop their torpedoes. Where were they? Had they already been released? Was the man in the crow's nest blind? Then the planes zoomed over the ship and away. The pilots hoicked them up, turned away and flew back.

The last three planes, at least, had recognized the *Sheffield*.

The excitement died down. The frantic zig-zagging had carried the cruiser farther away from the *Bismarck*. Captain Larcom now turned back in the direction of the enemy and ploughed through the sea after the German flagship.

Meanwhile Sir John was waiting for news of the air attack's success. The Admiral was uneasy. But only those close beside him noticed it, so controlled, so composed did he appear. He kept looking at his watch.

The other officers on the bridge did the same.

What was wrong? News of the attack should have reached them long ago. Was the weather too bad?

The *Bismarck*'s flak too lethal? Had she dodged too skilfully? Or – inconceivable though it seemed – had every single one of the planes fallen victim to the German anti-aircraft guns?

News came at last.

Sir James Somerville, Commander of Force H, radioed laconically : 'No hit.'

Admiral Tovey had no idea yet that the *Ark Royal*'s Swordfish had attacked one of their own ships.

The unhappy planes had meanwhile returned to the carrier. Only now was the disastrous mistake explained. The airmen were beside themselves.

'There's no harm done,' said Captain Maund. 'You're not to blame... Go and get something to eat and then be ready for another take-off.'

Once again chance intervened in the war at sea. How was it possible, thought Captain Maund, that the Swordfish were unable to destroy the *Sheffield*, which was far weaker than the *Bismarck*? That not one torpedo reached its target, although the pilots were able to take their time over aiming, because of the absence of flak? The torpedoes' modern magnetic pistols had failed. Captain Maund at once decided to go back to the well-tried contact pistols. He had the torpedoes changed. He was led to take this measure by the incredible and fortunately unsuccessful attack on one of their own ships.

It was the torpedoes armed with contact pistols that made possible the enemy's destruction, for the Swordfish were on the point of taking off for the second time. The carrier's deck canted in the heavy sea as the planes were refuelled. It was 7 p.m. Clouds were being driven along helter-skelter at a height of 600 feet above the water by a strong wind. Heavily disguised by their flying kit, the crews stood on the landing deck, vigorous youngsters burning to make good their mistake. Their cold determination was mixed with fear, a feeling none of the young airmen would have allowed to show for anything in the world. How many of them would come back? How many would be torn to shreds by enemy gunfire?

How many prayers would be said, how many mothers weep? This is what they were thinking about, although they strove with might and main to avoid it, although their pale faces were set in a ghastly smile. A deep breath, and they were off.

The duel with death had begun, the rendezvous with destiny, over which they had as little control as the young men on the other side against whom they were going to fire their deadly torpedoes.

The propellers swung. The engines whined into life. Heavily, cumbrously the machines rose from the deck and new off towards the foe. One of them was destined to land a hit in a million. A torpedo paralysed the *Bismarck*. A torpedo brought the beginning of the end, the end of the most modern battleship in the world....

The *Bismarck* was haunted by questions. What's going on? Where are we heading for? What are we doing? How long will this ghostly quiet last? The gnawing uncertainty lay heavily on the men in the gun turrets, the engine-rooms, the sick-bay, the magazines, the wireless cabins; it sneaked about the mess decks, settled in the officers' cabins, ground down the nerves of the 'holiday-makers', made the faces of the aircrews pale and set.

What was going on?

Two small black dots were circling over the German flagship out of range of her guns – enemy planes, like vultures following a doomed caravan. They would dis-appear for a few minutes, come back again, fly higher, drop down lower. It had been going on for hours.

It was late afternoon on 26 May, 1941, one and three-quarter days before the holocaust...

The men on the upper deck saw those tiny spiders up above them. They knew what they meant. No air-raid warning was sounded. A couple of enemy planes that kept out of firing range were no longer sufficient grounds for an alert on the *Bismarck*.

At the same time a tragi-comedy was being enacted in the skies. Independently of one another, a Catalina flying-boat and a Swordfish had made contact with the *Bismarck*. The Catalina radioed back: 'Being attacked by German fighter.'

The flying-boat swerved away through the clouds to escape the supposed enemy, and by so doing lost touch with the *Bismarck*.

For its part, the Swordfish mistook the flying-boat for a Focke-Wulf 200 and likewise beat a retreat. The two planes met again over the *Bismarck*, but spent more time watching one another than the German ship.

Meanwhile the latter's upper works were disguised.

The *Bismarck* was given an artificial funnel. The outline of the German battleship was altered with tin and cardboard to resemble that of the American battleship *Missouri*, in order to fool her pursuers. Not much hope was placed in this desperate piece of bluff.

Quite rightly.

The Swordfish were already on their way with their deadly cargo.

A few minutes more and the time had come.

Five minutes before the torpedo-planes attacked, Petty Officer Lindenberg was admitted to the sick-bay with a dental fistula. The left side of his face was grotesquely swollen. He couldn't speak, because of the pain, and took part in the conversation only by gestures. To his left lay Leading Seaman Knolle. His leg was in plaster and raised. He had fallen the previous day and broken his ankle. Opposite him was Schuze II, feverish with jaundice. The most cheerful of the patients was Able Seaman Burger, whose appendicitis operation, carried out only a few days ago, scarcely bothered him any more.

'Hullo,' he called, as Lindenberg was brought in. 'You're not very chatty. Man alive, where's your eye got to? Talk about an ugly mug! What the hell's bitten you?'

Lindenberg shook his fists at him half-heartedly and lay down on his bed.

'He hasn't much to say for himself,' went on Burger.

'At last there's a petty officer who keeps his trap shut,' added Knolle. 'Pity they're not all like that.'

'He can't kiss either.'

'Who's he supposed to kiss? You perhaps?'

'Pipe down,' said Schuze II.

'Did you hear that?' Knolle turned to Burger. The sick-bay Chinaman is talking... How do you like being a canary?'

Schuze II turned over with a groan.

Sick Berth Attendant Birner entered.

'Temperature time, gentlemen,' he said.

'Again?' expostulated Knolle. 'Why does a chap with a broken ankle have to have his temperature taken?'

'Regulations,' answered Birner. 'Come on, gentlemen, get a move on... You too. Petty Officer.'

'What happens if we go down?' asked Burger.

'Then you'll get a special treat. You'll be placed into a rubber dinghy and the Surgeon Commander will personally row you across the pond.'

"Struth, in that case we shan't get far.'

Sick Berth Attendant Birner collected the thermometers.

At that moment it happened. At that moment the sailors' flat-footed witticisms were abruptly silenced by the ringing of alarm bells.

O-n-e, t-w-o, t-h-r-e-e, f-o-u-r, f-i-v-e, shrilled the bells through the giant ship.

A brief pause.

O-n-e, t-w-o, t-h-r-e-e, f-o-u-r, f-i-v-e, came the warning signal again.

Again and again.

The sound went through and through them. Through their nerves. Through their heads, through their bodies. Eyes wavered. Everyone instinctively tried to jump out of bed. The Sick Berth Attendant forgot to enter the temperatures on the charts.

A Surgeon Lieutenant came running through the' sick-bay. There was a confused sound of shouting and sea-boots trampling over the armour plating.

Air-raid warning!

According to plan, the Swordfish from the *Ark Royal* flew to the *Sheffield*, which had been maintaining contact with the *Bismarck* for two hours. (The man in the cruiser's crow's-nest who first spotted the German flagship received £2 reward.) Planes and ships conversed by signals. The first formation of Swordfish, flying at a great height, reached their target.

At this moment the enemy planes were spotted by an observer on the *Bismarck*.

'Several enemy planes in sight,' he called out.

But the next instant the black dots on the horizon had vanished. Those responsible hesitated to sound the air-raid warning.

Able Seamen Rzonca and Junghans were standing on the upper deck. Rzonca was working on the catapulting apparatus of the aeroplanes. Junghans, whose battle station was in 'D' turret, was mine-spotting. They both heard the aircraft-spotter's report at the same time. They stared up at the sky and saw nothing.

'He's dreaming,' shouted Junghans.

'No, he saw seagulls,' answered Rzonca.

Tension relaxed, dissolved into laughter and relief. They were gulls – not aircraft!

But at this very moment the Swordfish, high in the clouds, were forming up for the decisive attack on the *Bismarck*.

The first sub-flight came hurtling down.

The air-raid warning sounded.

'All hands to action stations!'

Everyone raced to the hatches. In a few seconds they were closed down. So quickly, so suddenly that Able Seaman Rzonca was left standing on the upper deck, an unwilling eye-witness of the hellish attack.

Flak blazed from every barrel, supported by the medium guns. Despite the hail of fire, the biplanes came tearing in from port and starboard. Five, eight, ten machines. From every side simultaneously, in carefully planned confusion.

All at once Able Seaman Behnke was beside Rzonca.

'Come into the shelter,' he yelled at his shipmate. 'I didn't have time to get down below either.'

The *Bismarck* was encircled by a girdle of shell-bursts. Could one of the enemy planes break through the flak? Had any pilot enough reckless courage to fly through this barrage of destruction? Had he a chance?

There

the first Swordfish burst into flames and blew up in mid-air. The wreckage plunged blazing into the sea. But behind it came another machine. It was quite close already. For a moment it seemed to be hanging motionless in the air. At this second it released its torpedo. Torpedo track starboard!

They began firing at the torpedo. One shot landed. It exploded, sending up a tall column of water.

The British were coming from all sides, breaking with frantic bravery through the curtain of gunfire.

Rzonca and Behnke raced to a 1-inch gun, handed ammunition, threw themselves under cover, watched the automatic gun empty its magazines, saw the trail of the tracer bullets, saw one of the machines catch fire, watched the red-hot barrel of the gun being changed just as a fresh Swordfish zoomed in.

My God, will it never end? thought Rzonca. Fancy me being here with the flak batteries of all places. What guts the flak boys have got! They're firing like madmen. They're firing as they did in the Baltic during the working-up, when they aimed their guns at a drogue drawn by an aeroplane. If they hit it they got a crate of beer. Now it's a matter of life or death. Life instead of a crate of beer....

'Come on! Faster!' bawled the gun-captain.

Torpedoes were hissing towards them from all directions. The *Bismarck* zig-zagged at full speed. She dodged three or four slippery eels.

Then a machine flew in from aft and released its projectile in the midst of the raging anti-aircraft fire.

The torpedo entered the water with a slap and churned the waves towards the *Bismarck*'s armoured skin.

The guns were turned on it. The shots fell short, over, to one side or the other.

Good God, aim better! More accurately! Keep calm! Concentrate! You've got plenty of time. Another fifteen seconds, another ten. For God's sake blow it up!

Rzonca was standing on the stern deck, ten or twelve feet from the AA battery. He saw the torpedo speeding towards them.

'Come on,' he yelled to Behnke. 'Over to the other side!'

They raced a few paces to starboard and threw themselves down.

Then came the explosion.

The whole stern shuddered. Next moment the *Bismarck* veered off to port in a narrow arc and then steamed on in a circle.

The steering gear had been hit.

The rudder was jammed fast.

Make smoke! But the smoke plant was out of action.

'Don't just stand there,' an officer bellowed at Rzonca and Behnke. 'Go and see what's wrong.'

The smoke plant was right astern. The two Able Seamen raised the cover. The connexions were bent, the armatures buckled. Behnke climbed down and shone his torch into the tangle.

'Be careful,' Rzonca called after him.

The same instant he saw a 15-inch gun trained round until its barrel was pointing directly aft. Rzonca saw the mouth right in front of him, pulled Behnke up and jumped to one side. The gun flashed. The two seamen were flung to the deck by the blast.

The *Bismarck* was crippled. The rudder was stuck at almost 20 degrees to port. Nor could the flagship be steered by her screws. They must also be damaged. The *Bismarck* turned round in a circle.

At last the stern was hidden in smoke. From smoke buoys.

Once more the aeroplanes came on. One Swordfish tried to drop a torpedo straight on to the deck. It attacked from the bows.

The 15-inch turret fired.

An explosion in mid-air and the plane had vanished. A direct hit.

At last the planes turned away.

Damage-control parties went into action. Divers went down to the steering gear. They worked frantically but unavailingly. An announcement boomed out all over the ship.

'Steering gear damaged. Repairs in progress. Prospect that the damage can be made good.'

When the divers came back on deck again and made their reports they were exhausted. The icy water had taken it out of them. The hopelessness of the task broke their courage. The damage was beyond repair. The whole position beyond hope. They reported the situation to the officers. The officers ordered them not to make their observations known to the men.

While confidence and optimism were still being ladled out to the crew, the *Bismarck* was sending despairing radio messages out into the ether.

At 8.54 p.m. Admiral Lütjens reported: 'Under attack by enemy carrier aircraft.'

At 9.05: 'Ship no longer manoeuvrable. Approximate position 47° 40' N, 14° 15" W. Hit by torpedo aft.'

At 9.15 : 'Hit by torpedo amidships.'

At 9.17 the Commander-in-Chief German Western Naval Command in France, radioed back:

'U-boat reports one battleship, one aircraft carrier at approx. 47° 50' N, 16° 50' W, 115°, proceeding at high speed.'

Barely an hour later Western Command made radio contact with the *Bismarck* again and informed the German flagship that every available German U-boat had been ordered to her assistance...

From the first second on, Lieutenant-Commander Werner Nobis refused to delude himself. Henceforth navigation of the *Bismarck* was in the hands of the sea, the storm-lashed, cruel sea. The ship was drifting almost without a will of its own – drifting towards the enemy. The British merely had to position themselves. They merely had to muster their units. There would be no real battle at all.

It was execution that faced the *Bismarck*, not battle...

Night brought a dubious respite. It fed the thousandfold fear of death. It paralysed nerves and at the same time whipped them up. Thought became torture. Hope stupidity. Stupidity hope. Hands shook, eyes stared vacantly, stomachs struck, voices failed. And thoughts returned. Thoughts of Deina...

The more hopeless the situation became, the closer came the girl from Oporto. There was no escape.

Neither from death – nor from Deina....

That night in Portugal, when Werner Nobis stood outside Deina's front door, when he kissed the girl, when he wanted to ask for money and clothing and only words of love came to his lips, in that bright moonlight night he could have changed everything to the better.

'What a sight you look!' exclaimed Deina. 'Come inside and wash yourself.'

'What about your mother?'

'My mother will understand.'

He followed her. He saw her slender figure and he forgot, while her nearness made him feel hot and cold, happy and unhappy at the same time, that he was a German officer on the run from an internment camp. He forgot that he was running away to Germany. Running away into the war. That he was trying to desert from the world of peace, because he imagined he had to do his so-called duty.

Then he was sitting beside her. The door to the balcony stood open. Crickets were chirping. A radio played softly. A bottle of cognac stood on the table. The light was out.

What need was there for light tonight?

For the first time he was alone with her. For the first time in his life he was really in love. But this one and only real love had to remain unreal. This was what war demanded. This was what the code of honour of a German naval officer demanded. And Werner Nobis believed he had to comply with this demand.

'You've escaped?'

'Yes.'

She stroked his hair.

What a scoundrel I am, thought Nobis. Why did I come and see her again? Everything was going well. You don't need money in this country. And a drill suit is enough. Who cares about a runaway German internee here? Who bothers here about anything except the sun, laughter, peace, wine and the little bit of work necessary to enjoy it all? To live, breathe and be free in a happy, contented, peaceful country...

'You'll stay with me, won't you?' asked Deina.

'Yes,' said Nobis.

'He was lying. He wanted to lie. Good God, how lovely a lie can be! It can bewitch two or three hours, turn them into an eternity and enable us to forget that they are divided into seconds.

'Are you hungry?' she enquired.

'No, not in the least.'

She smiled. Werner Nobis couldn't see it, but he felt it.

'Do you feel as happy as I do?'

'Yes, Deina.'

Then everything is all right,' she whispered. 'And it will stay like that... My God, how glad I am that you've seen sense at last. I had almost given up hope. Hadn't you?'

'I felt just the same. After you had left the hospital I didn't know if I was standing on my head or my heels.'

'But now you know?'

The night stretched out its arms to them. It brought them together, made them happy.

A thousand tender caresses were still hovering about the room, when thoughts began to assail Werner Nobis once more. The demands of unreasonable reason. The imperative of brutal, ice-cold duty...

Deina lay beside him, sleeping. She was still smiling happily in her sleep. The first pale rays of dawn touched her face. Nobis gazed at her, again and again. She seemed to notice it as she dozed, for she murmured something and turned over to the other side.

I must go, Werner Nobis told himself. There's nothing for it. I must go.

But the next moment he believed the opposite.

I must stay. I must stay with Deina. I can't leave her. Hell, I don't want to abandon her. Under no circumstances. Not for anything in the world...

Not for anything in the world?

Now he was here on the *Bismarck*, the most powerful battleship in the world, preparing himself for death. Preparing himself to die in four, five, perhaps seven hours. This time he would not make the wrong decision. There was nothing left to decide. It would all happen automatically.

He need only stick to the post to which duty had nailed him fast. Then the moment would come...

The *Bismarck*'s plight was still totally unknown to the British. They did not know that her end was draw-ing near with giant strides. The leader of the first sub-flight of planes radioed:

'Probably no hits.'

For the second time this report reached Admiral John Tovey. For the last time that day, for night had fallen. It forbade further aerial attacks. Now he could only send his fastest units, the destroyers, after the German flagship.

The *Ark Royal*'s Swordfish were back. Only one machine was missing.

How was Sir John to know that the radio signal 'Probably no hits' referred only to the formation made up of the first three planes to attack? He was still several miles away from the *Bismarck*'s position. His units' oil supplies permitted no further operations. The ships had still to return to their bases. Moreover, they faced the danger of attack by German U-boats. This meant a zig-zag course at full speed. And that used up a lot of oil.

When Commodore Blackman of the *Edinburgh* heard the radio mesage from the Swordfish, he immediately steered for home. He passed the *Sheffield* and *Ark Royal* repeatedly in the course of the day and must be quite close to the *Bismarck*, but he could not make her out. Now it was too late for the *Edinburgh*. She was down to her last drop of oil. The cruiser would be lucky if she succeeded in making port.

That was the gloomy prospect on the British side, when Admiral John Tovey shook his head in perplexity over an apparently unintelligible report from the *Sheffield*, which was still shadowing the *Bismarck*.

'*Bismarck* changing course. 340° north-north-west.'

What did that mean? Was the *Bismarck* trying to shake off the troublesome shadower? Even while the Swordfish were attacking, she had fired a few salvoes at the *Sheffield*, scoring direct hits on the hull. Three killed and twelve wounded by splinters. The *Sheffield* at once put on speed and made smoke.

Her radar scanner was destroyed.

Was Captain Larcom's report of the *Bismarck*'s course based on a miscalculation?

To begin with. Admiral Tovey was convinced of it. Then the Swordfish landed on the *Ark Royal*. The crews swore they had seen at least two torpedoes hit the mark. Now a radio signal came in from a flying-boat.

It confirmed that the *Bismarck* was steering a northerly course.

Was Captain Larcom right after all?

More reports came in. They all confirmed that the *Bismarck* was heading north-north-west.

She was heading straight for the enemy squadrons. There could be no doubt about it.

What did it mean?

There could be only one explanation, an explanation that delighted the British and spelt disaster for the Germans. Admiral Lütjens's flagship was no longer manoeuvrable. She was forced to steer this suicidal course against the sea, because her steering gear was smashed.

Sir John acted at once. He put his flotilla on to a southerly course. He made straight for the *Bismarck*. Battle must inevitably be joined during the next few hours.

Commodore Blackman of the *Edinburgh* quickly realized the new position, snapped his fingers at his fuel worries and turned back towards the enemy.

Then, as though sent from heaven, five destroyers led by Captain Vian came steaming up. That very night they carried out a daredevil attack...

That was the situation, the *Bismarck*'s hopeless situation, in the late evening of 26 May, 1941. Around this time Admiral Lütjens sent out three radio messages in quick succession.

11.40 p.m.: 'Ship unmanoeuvrable. We shall fight to the last shell. Long live the Führer. Fleet Commander."

11.58 p.m.: 'To the Führer of the German Reich, Adolf Hitler. Believing in you, my Führer, we shall fight to the last and in unshakable confidence in Germany's victory. Fleet Commander.'

11.59 p.m.: 'Armaments and engines still intact. But ship cannot be steered with the engines. Fleet Commander.'

Meanwhile a devilish guest had settled in the *Bismarck* – the dread of death.

Rumours that the steering gear. was beyond repair came thick and fast. Admiral Lütjens put an end to them by confirming them.

Everyone knew what that meant.

Everyone had a few hours in which to get used to the idea.

Everyone looked for a way out. And everyone despaired of finding one. Everyone knew that Fate had changed Admiral Lütjen's motto from 'Victory or Death' to 'Victory and Death'.

The 2,402 men of the *Bismarck* had victory over the *Hood* behind them.

But death was still to come...

That night, which provided the last respite before the holocaust, the dread of death was abroad on the invulnerable yet fatally injured *Bismarck*. All-powerful and brutal, it took possession of the mammoth ship, gripped the lower decks, dominated the engine-rooms, invaded the fire-control towers, lurked in the officers' cabins, cast its shadow over the bridges.

Men in over-heated rooms shivered with cold, men on the upper decks sweated in the cold night air. Dread of death found expression in a thousand forms, under a thousand twisted masks. Senses, nerves and hearts vibrated to the merciless tune of this eerie, monstrous, inhuman spirit. What the

2,402 men of the *Bismarck* went through, what they felt, hoped and feared, during these bitter and despairing hours of night was worse than the end itself. For the end was quick.

For most of them, anyhow...

Only a few days ago these young men had entered the war at sea with laughing faces, youthful optimism and a considerable portion of indifference. Beneath a mantle of patriotism slumbered their hopes, fears, confidence and faith. Faith in victory. Which of them ever thought that their victory meant death for the others? Which of them thought that in the hands of the mass-murderer war, victory and defeat, death and life, were a matter of blind and bloody chance?

Which of them knew the taste of death?

Knew how lonely death can be?

How many times you have to die before you are dead?

How resolution wavers before this strangling, throttling, icy, boiling-hot dread of death? How scoffers pray, strong men weep, ranks vanish, cowards become heroes and heroes cowards? How the vague, traditional, much-extolled notions of manly courage, comradeship and a hero's death dissolve, disappear, slink away?

Sub-Lieutenant Peters sat in his cabin writing. Rapidly, hurriedly, nervously, page after page. At school he always had poor marks for German because his compositions were too short. Later, when he went to sea, his mother complained in every letter about how little he wrote to her. To be exact, apart from a few disconnected, commonplace expressions of affection that had degenerated into meaningless cliches, his letters contained only requests, requests for cigarettes, money, eatables, things he wanted done. His letters were brief and to the point – like naval reports.

Now, facing death and tormented by fear, he found words. Words to his mother that had never passed his lips before. He wrote at a tremendous speed, with an obsessive energy, as though trying to make up for all his omissions of the past. The one-sided dialogue with his mother was a flight from this barbaric fear, from dread, from death.

This letter never reached the lonely old woman. Sub-Lieutenant Peters temporarily saved the lives of two of his shipmates and then died. 'In heroic fulfilment of his duty to Führer, nation and Fatherland,' it said in the newspaper some weeks later.

How many were writing, how many praying, how many hoping, how many cursing, how many weeping?

Suddenly everyone was afraid of being alone. Suddenly everyone turned to his shipmates, as though they, who were throttled by the same dread,

Kapitän zur See *Ernst Lindemann* (1894-1941)

Admiral *Günther Lütjens (1889-1941)*

Korvettenkapitän *(Ing.) Walter Lehmann* (1903-1941).

Korvettenkapitän *Adalbert Schneider* (1904-1941).

HMS Suffolk

Prinz Eugen

Pocket Battleship Gneisenau

Bismarck

HMS Hood.

Swordfish flying from the deck of HMS Victorious.

HMS Norfolk.

Vice-Admiral Sir James Somerville and Captain Maundem, commander of the Ark Royal.

The Bismarck firing a salvo at HMS Hood.

Admiral Sir John Tovey on his Flag Ship HMS King George V.

HMS Ark Royal.

HMS Rodney.

HMS Sheffield.

Philip Vian, Commander of HMS Cossack.

could afford protection against his own fear. At all costs avoid being alone, perhaps the others could help, perhaps somebody could think of a way out.

The ratings had finally learnt that the *Bismarck*'s steering gear was beyond repair. Everybody knew what that meant.

Then came the next announcement over the loud-speakers:

'Free issue of all stores. Everyone may take what he wants.'

Ten minutes later again: 'Ship's stores open... Canteen goods for the taking.'

The men heard and understood, but they did not react. What use were greedy hands, when the stomach was on strike? Canteen goods! The dream of every fighting-man, the ray of light in the monotony of barrack life, the signal for high spirits. Free issue of stores! Ham in tinfoil, chocolate in tins, tinned fruit, meat in its own gravy, cheese in tubes, cigarettes in huge packets, sweets in cellophane. As much as you wanted, as much as you could carry away! An inexhaustible supply. The rations for months issued in a few hours. Shaving-lotion, *eau de Cologne*, shaving brushes, hair cream, pocket knives, lighters, combs, tooth brushes, fountain pens. Everybody could take what he wanted. As much as he wanted. Free. You didn't even have to sign for the things. Death would foot the bill.

Leading Seaman Link had got hold of a watch. Lauchs of a bottle of brandy, although brandy was expressly excluded from the list of free goods. Moessmer was eating pineapple from a tin. Hengst was plastering his hair with *eau de Cologne*. The others sat dully around. On the flap-shelf lay rolled ham. They were sickened by rolled ham, by brandy, by Link's new first-class Swiss-made watch. When the big hand had completed its circle nine times it would be time for his wedding by proxy. His wedding to Else.

But before then it was all over. For Link, anyhow.

Lauchs offered his bottle round.

'Drink, mates, I've got another one put by.'

Only Moessmer took a gulp.

'It goes fine with pineapple,' he said, opening a second tin.

'Stop guzzling that muck,' Hinrichs bawled at him. 'You'll only make all the worse mess in your pants.'

'I've got armour-plated guts,' retorted Moessmer. 'Why don't you have some grub?... Because you're afraid of catting? Go on, stuff yourselves. It's on the Fatherland.'

He took another pull at Lauchs's bottle.

'The gratitude of the Fatherland,' he said. 'Down the hatch.'

'You lousy bastard,' Drechsel yelled at him. 'Keep your trap shut. I can't stand your natter.'

'They can't simply let us go to the bottom,' cried Pollack suddenly. 'They must do something.'

'They'll do something all right,' replied Lauchs. He put the half-empty bottle to his lips. 'They'll make speeches. They'll hold memorial services in the schools. And when the war's over they'll put up a memorial, on which the sparrows will have a good time.'

'You lousy bastard,' swore Drechsel.

"They'll send you a special coffin,' retorted Lauchs, 'by air mail.'

'But we've plenty of U-boats,' said Moessmer. 'What do you think will happen to the Tommies when they attack us? There'll be thirty or forty of them all at once. Do you think they're stupid? Do you think they built the *Bismarck* so the Tommies could blow her to pieces?'

'Don't talk daft,' Hengst interrupted him. 'What do you imagine U-boats can do against battleships? You know very well the torpedoes just bounce off.'

'Well, what about us?' snapped Hengst. 'It was a torpedo that put us in this mess.'

'Don't work yourselves up,' broke in Hinrichs. 'There are planes too. The Tommies will fair belt when they see the Junker 88s coming!'

'They're much too far away. Besides, they've got to get back again. You don't imagine they'll go into the drink for us, do you?'

'They'll use auxiliary tanks,' said Pollack.

'Go on, kid yourselves as long as you can,' scoffed Lauchs. 'Why don't you have a drink? It's easier to die with a belly full of booze.'

'I've all I can stand from him,' roared Pollack. 'I'm going to swipe him in the kisser!'

Lauchs laughed. Loudly and coarsely. His eyes were already glazed. He had bought himself off from the fear of death for a few hours with drink. For the time 'being he didn't care about anything. He felt warm, almost hot. The others were muzzy-headed and babbled about aeroplanes and U-boats, trying to blind themselves to the atrocious truth with words. They envied him. Envied him his gastric nerves, that could still stand drink. Envied him his nerves in general.

'I'm going to be sick,' said Moessmer. Green in the face, he jumped up and ran to the bulkhead.

'Mind you aim straight!' shouted Lauchs.

All at once there was silence. Everyone looked at everybody else. Everyone saw the others' anxious, feverish, agitated eyes. Everyone saw the others' hands shaking. Everyone heard the drone of the engines. Everyone thought of himself, his home, his wife, of leave, of death, of being sick, of flight, of the U-boats, the aeroplanes, of the shells, of the sea, of drowning, of his children, of pineapples in tins. Suddenly they all looked at Link's new watch. Suddenly they all stopped talking. The silence became torment, agony, despair. Dread of dying flitted across the pale, unshaven, tormented faces.

Of a sudden everyone waited, hoped, wagered on the drunken chatter of Able Seaman Lauchs. But the man with the iron gastric nerves said nothing. The fear of death had sobered him. His Dutch courage turned into nausea.

At this moment long past midnight the silence was rent by the loudspeaker. Anxious eyes sought the invisible voice that was reading a message from the supreme German warlord – the man who was driving them, a nation, a whole world to war, to destruction.

'I thank you in the name of the whole German people. All Germany is with you. What can be done will be done. The exemplary manner in which you have carried out your duty will fortify our nation in its fight for life. Adolf Hitler.'

Hitler's message was immediately repeated.

'So now you know,' commented Pfeiffer.

'Heil Hitler!' retorted Hengst.

Then there was silence again. A ghostly silence. A deathly silence. Everyone had an opportunity to think his own thoughts about the end...

Meanwhile the British fleet was advancing according to plan. The airmen who had braved death to launch their torpedoes landed on the *Ark Royal* with empty tanks and reported unanimously that after their attack the *Bismarck* had made two full circles and finished up with her bows pointing northward.

At 12.59 a.m. on the fateful 27 May 1941, Admiral Sir John Tovey learnt of the sensational change in the situation.

Now, hours before the final battle, he addressed the following message to the crew of his flagship. *King George V*:

'The sinking of the *Bismarck* may have an effect on the war out of all proportion to the loss to the enemy of one battleship. May God be with you and grant you victory.'

In the shadow of the night destruction began.

Sir John steered a south-westerly course. The *Bismarck* was coming to meet him of its own accord along a semi-circular course. Force H, part of the Mediterranean Fleet under the command of Sir James Somerville, received orders to take up a position not less than 20 miles to the southward of the *Bismarck*. If necessary, the torpedo aircraft of the *Ark Royal*, which belonged to this squadron, could intervene in the final stages of the battle from close at hand. The *Renown* had orders from Admiral Tovey not to take part in the battle, to avoid any possible risk of her being confused with the German flagship. In Tovey's opinion *King George V* and *Rodney* would be capable of destroying the enemy on their own.

At the eleventh hour the British forces were further strengthened by the heavy cruiser *Dorsetshire* under Captain Martin. He had been escorting a convoy and when he learnt of the *Bismarck*'s position was about 600 miles west of Cape Finisterre. Captain Martin left the convoy to proceed on its own, veered east-north-east and steamed towards the *Bismarck* at full speed, disregarding his fuel shortage.

Night had grown darker still. The stars where hiding behind heavy clouds. Fate postponed the decision till dawn.

But even now, in the small hours of 27 May 1941, as first light came through the cold mist of early morning to herald a day marked for all time with a sea of blood in the annals of the German Navy, a naval attack was launched that resembled those of bygone days...

Captain Vian led the death or glory squadron – five British destroyers that raced out of the pitch-dark, icy night to attack the most modern battleship in the world. Five faster vessels against one more powerful one. Five Davids against one Goliath. Five crews braving death against one crew condemned to death. Throughout one endless, ice-cold night. Again and again. Torpedo after torpedo. Salvo after salvo. The paralysed colossus fired from every barrel to score her last victory before the holocaust...

Aboard the *Cossack*, Captain Vian gave his orders briefly, coolly and intensely. He had gained world fame at the beginning of 1940 by his attack on the *Altmark*. During the night of 16 to 17 February he took his ship into Norwegian territorial waters, boarded a German auxiliary vessel and rescued the British prisoners she was carrying. After this action Vian became the hero of the British destroyer fleet.

Vian now acted without orders. He didn't hesitate for a second. With fearful courage he drove the destroyers *Cossack*, *Sikh*, *Maori*, *Zulu* and *Piorun* into the line of fire of the *Bismarck*, whose steering gear was smashed, but whose 15-inch guns still fired accurately...

Take up positions for attack! Out of range of the *Bismarck*. *Maori*, *Sikh*, *Piorun* and *Zulu* formed a wide square round the German flagship. The *Cossack* was shadowing from astern. 'Positions taken up,' came the report to Captain Vian at 11.24 p.m.

A synchronized torpedo attack from five sides. A textbook manoeuvre.

But the churning sea cared little for lessons learned at the naval staff college. Wind, waves, bad visibility and inadequate radar equipment split up the flotilla before it was on the enemy.

The *Cossack* raced on at full speed. Her bows sliced through the waves.

'Arm torpedoes!'

'Range four miles.'

'Get closer!'

The engines laboured as though they would blow up at any moment. Nothing in sight yet. Damn!

'Closer still!'

A battleship is bigger than a destroyer. Its outline should loom earlier out of the darkness of the night. During those few seconds, between spotting the enemy and being spotted by him, the destroyers' torpedoes must splash into the water and hiss towards their target at 50 m.p.h.

Where the hell was the *Bismarck*, where was she hiding, where was she lying in wait, in which direction was she training her guns, when would she fire?

Not yet, the men on the *Cossack* told themselves, that was quite impossible. They can't see us before we spot her. Just keep calm, keep steady. This wasn't the first time. Things had gone well often enough before. It would be all right this time. Then home. Leave. Then another mission perhaps. Away from this tub, which a single direct hit from the *Bismarck* would blow to smithereens. Which was bound to go to the bottom one day. On a day they hoped they wouldn't see.

Seconds became torturers. Mouths were dry. Food lay heavy on the stomach. Shirts clung clammily to the body. Thought was switched off. Only feelings, this ghastly mixture of fear and hope, could not be switched off.

Hands were on levers and knobs, ears listening to the voice tube for orders.

Then there was a roar.

Impossible! It must be imagination!

It was not imagination. Huge fountains of water rose close on the *Cossack*'s beam. Very close.

A gun fired.

The sound of impact.

Fragments of shell. A wireless aerial was blown away.

'Turn away!' roared Captain Vian. 'Zig-zag! Out of the line of fire! Back! Reform!'

Once again they had got away. Once again. But the night was not over. Not by a long chalk. Would it be their last night? Hell no, of course it wouldn't, it couldn't be.

What has happened? wondered Captain Vian. How could the *Bismarck* fire at us before we were even within sighting distance?

There was only one solution, he believed. The enemy was firing by radar. The *Bismarck* was the first German battleship whose guns could be aimed in the dark.

Destroyers hadn't a chance. To aim their torpedoes they would have to get within range of the deadly radar-controlled fire. Not a hope!

That meant giving up.

But not for Captain Vian...

Eight minutes later the *Zulu* was under fire from the *Bismarck*. One salvo straddled the destroyer to port and starboard. Then came the next. Closer still. Three wounded. An officer and two ratings. The *Zulu* turned away, escaped, but lost contact with the *Bismarck* as she did so and only reestablished it half an hour later.

The *Maori* found herself within range of the *Bismarck*'s, guns. *Sikh*, too, had to turn back without having released her torpedoes. For half an hour all the destroyers lost contact with the *Bismarck*. Worse still, they lost touch with each other. By chance *Cossack* met *Zulu* and *Piorun*.

In any case, Captain Vian could no longer conduct a synchronized attack. He gave the order for his vessels to assail the German battleship individually. While the *Bismarck* was directing her fire at one destroyer, the others were to creep up on her. The witches' sabbath of this night had only just begun. Captain Vian repeated his daring attacks time after time.

All night long.

Had the destroyers a chance? Wasn't it madness to rush into the lethal gunfire? To come within torpedo range? Not till the following morning would it be known how many of the five destroyers had survived their suicidal onslaughts...

Alarm bells shattered the dull, stubborn waiting-aboard the *Bismarck*. Already? The men stared at one another. Couldn't they have waited with the execution till morning? Were they coming already with their crushingly superior forces?

No. They were only destroyers, the enemy's vanguard. Ridiculous! Destroyers against a battleship! Torpedoes against chrome-nickel-steel walls!

Time had lost all meaning. Was that the second or third wave of attacking destroyers? A star shell blazed across the *Bismarck*, tearing a hole in the night and casting a ghostly light on the scene. Two torpedoes raced towards them, but shot past well in front of the bows.

That damned rudder! Ponderously, unwillingly the colossus reacted. With a tired movement she swung round to port. Broadside on to the invisible enemy.

Then there was calm again. Quite suddenly. Once more the oppression, fear and horror. Once more the empty chatter. Once more the silence.

The adversary had vanished into the night and would not return till morning. No one on the *Bismarck* suspected yet that the night battle was far from over.

Commander Schneider, the *Bismarck*'s First Gunnery Officer, was ordered to report to Admiral Lütjens. For the last forty-eight hours the Admiral had not left the bridge. He looked pale and frail. As always, he spoke coldly, impersonally, in short sharp sentences, as though the *Bismarck* were on manoeuvres, not fighting for her life.

Was he immune to the fear of death? Was the abstract tradition of the naval officer stronger than the dread of dying? The uniform more powerful than natural feelings? Than the instinct of self-preservation? Than the ultimate question: For whose benefit is all this? Did it ever occur to him that he and his crew were only dying to uphold a political system which the majority of German naval officers inwardly rejected? Why, after all, did he wear at his side the 'Imperial' dagger, not the dagger with the swastika?

'Commander Schneider reporting, sir,' said Schneider.

The Admiral straightened up. He spoke briefly and tersely.

'The Führer has awarded you the Knight's Cross for the sinking of the *Hood*... I congratulate you.'

'Thank you, sir.' Handshake. About turn. Commander Schneider left the bridge.

A minute later the crew was informed over the loudspeakers that an officer of the *Bismarck* had been awarded the Knight's Cross...

Only for five hours. But that wasn't mentioned.

Hearty congratulations, thought Lieutenant-Commander Werner Nobis bitterly. He was sitting with two other officers in the chart-room. Strictly speaking, they were all off watch. What navigating could they do on a ship that was no longer manoeuvrable? Wind and waves were now steering the *Bismarck*.

Thoughts, too, followed their own course. During these hours between living and dying, every man aboard the *Bismarck* was now at the mercy of memory.

Nobis was thinking of Deina.

Everyone on board had a Deina somewhere...

Deina was sleeping peacefully, a happy smile on her face. Her hands were folded, as if from an unconscious desire to express her gratitude. Her pretty young face was flushed, fresh and beautiful. The tender exchanges of the night still seemed to be present in the room.

The caresses. The spoken and unspoken words. The wishes, the protestations, the hopes. The happiness....

The cool air of morning was wafted into the room from the sea. On the horizon the young day was taking over from the night. Oporto was still asleep. Far away, in the harbour, the first workmen were gathering.

To go or to stay? War or peace? To die or to love?

As to dying, that's nonsense, thought Nobis, the German lieutenant in flight from a Portuguese internment camp. Only the unlucky ones die. I shan't be unlucky.

Peace is beautiful, wonderful. But there is no peace, when there's a war on, when your own nation is at war. It would be glorious to stay, so glorious that it cannot be put into words. But is it possible to stay?

Does not war forbid it? Would there not come a day when one would stand ashamed before one's parents, one's brothers, one's friends, oneself, all those who had endured the inferno, had overcome it and emerged victorious?

But suppose they were not victorious?

Not victorious? Rubbish! You only had to read the newspapers, even the newspapers of a neutral country.

Nobis looked at Deina. God, he besought, make her wake up, now, this moment; then it would all be over, then there would be no more reflection, no demands of conscience, or what Nobis took for conscience. There would be no more escape from those eyes, those arms, that love. He would have to stay here. There would be no alternative. To hell with the war! Whether they won or lost, whether they were victorious or defeated. What did it matter to him? He had done his duty. His boat had been destroyed, blown to pieces by a bomb. The others, the dead, couldn't get back into the war either.

He gazed at Deina. She must wake up any minute. A sleeper always wakes up when you stare at him. Now!

No. She went on sleeping. Perhaps she was just dreaming of their common future, which they had painted for one another again and again during the hours that were past. Hours in which he had lied – and yet hoped that he might not be lying...

I can't go, Nobis tormented himself. Not now. Not today. Tomorrow perhaps. The war can wait a day. But would Nobis be able to go tomorrow? Would he ever be able to go, if he spent another day with Deina?

She was still asleep. She turned over a little, so that Nobis could see her face even more clearly. He need only stretch out his hand to it and she would wake. She would ask him what was wrong. He would throw his arms round her, kiss her, and the haunting spectre of escape and war would be exorcized for ever. Never to return. For both of us, Nobis told himself.

For us favoured children of war.

Day drew even nearer. The sun rose timidly in the east. It must be now. Now or never.

Nobis sprang out of bed. There was a tiny muffled sound. A last chance. No, there was no chance. Deina slept.

He stood in the doorway. Good God, what an awakening hers would be! Perhaps she would reach out for him sleepily. Perhaps she would whisper tender words while still half asleep.

I'll write to her, Nobis thought. I'll explain to her. I couldn't have made her understand now in any case. Besides, I couldn't have gone on speaking once she looked at me. Of what avail would my words have been against her eyes?

For a second his whole being seemed drawn into a knot. He felt the pain as something almost physical. He went without looking round again. He sneaked out of the house, he walked as though in a dream, a trance, with a final burst of devilish, useless determination. He ran away, it hurt and... he felt ashamed.

For the first hour he ran blindly on, wherever the road took him, without stopping to think, without any clear idea of where he was going, just forward. Forward – that meant back to Germany.

Then he imagined he could see her in front of him and hear her voice.

'You're going to stay with me?'

'Yes.'

'Are you happy?'

'Yes.'

'Then everything's all right.'

Then everything's all right...

She must be awake now, must have noticed that he had stolen away. Now she would be crying, cursing him, hating him. And he loved her!

He stopped and took his bearings. By chance he had run in the right direction. Eastwards. Now he only had to go straight ahead to the east and he would reach the Spanish frontier. Once again a lorry gave him a lift. He sat in the driver's cabin. They seemed to be in no hurry to catch him. There is never any hurry about anything in Portugal. And what did it matter to the Portuguese whether he got back to Germany? Why should they put themselves out over an escaped internee? He wasn't the first and certainly wouldn't be the last. And there were just as many escapes from the left-hand wing of the internment camp as from the right – from the British as from the German side.

The lorry-driver ate a piece of bread and sausage. Nobis must have looked hungrily at his fingers. The man broke his bread in two with a laugh and gave Nobis half. Then the lorry reached its destination and Nobis had to climb out. He continued for a while on foot. Then another lorry picked him up. Then a bit further on foot. For two days, living on other people's pity, on their patience and tact. For no one asked him who he was. No one seemed to take any interest in him. Everyone was bound to notice that there was something fishy about him. Anyone could see he was a foreigner.

He rested a little way from the frontier with no idea of how to get across illegally. But he managed it with an unfailing instinct. He was in Spain. Also a neutral country. But this neutrality looked different from the Portuguese. When he passed through a town he simply enquired after a German family. He told them he had escaped and unhesitatingly accepted money.

In this way he reached Madrid and reported to the German embassy. At first he was regarded with suspicion. Perhaps they took him for a secret agent. He had to wait for days while enquiries were made in Germany. Then the officials became friendly. He was given everything he asked for – a passport and a ticket to Germany.

They were already waiting for him with slaps on the back. He was decorated and promoted. Six weeks' home leave. For six weeks he trotted round the little Silesian town, allowing himself to be slapped on the back, though he didn't feel comfortable about it. But after all, he had done his duty, he told himself with simple pride. During the night, however, when he thought of Deina, this simple pride tasted bitter.

Then the Navy took him again. They gave him a free choice of where to report. 'Anyone who has twice gone down in a little tub has only one wish: to be on a big ship, if possible the biggest – the *Bismarck*.'

Training. Another course. Transfer to the *Bismarck*. Working-up. Trials in the Baltic. Then the time had come. The *Bismarck* put to sea from Gotenhafen on her first sortie.

It's a mere seven days since we left Gotenhafen, thought Nobis, what an eternity. Now he was sitting uselessly at the chart table waiting for the end. What was it he said in Portugal? It's only the unlucky ones who die.

Well, now he, Lieutenant-Commander Werner Nobis, was one of the unlucky ones.

Would he ever see Deina again? Just once? Just to explain to her, just to tell her how he cursed the decision he had reached that morning?

A salvo from the 15-inch turret interrupted his thoughts.

Was that the answer?

The British destroyers were attacking again. The witches' cauldron was beginning to seethe once more...

Hidden by the night, urged on by their orders, located by the enemy's radar, the five destroyers launched a fresh assault on the *Bismarck*. With icy resolve, *Cossack*, *Sikh*, *Piorun*, *Maori* and *Zulu* darted arrow-swift and nimble towards the uncontrollable German flagship – simultaneously, in carefully planned confusion, from port to starboard, fore and aft – from all sides.

Zulu was closest to the enemy. Commander Graham came in from astern, veered to starboard to assail the *Bismarck*. Everything okay so far. Range 6,000 yards. The last ounce was got out of the engines. Pitching and rolling, the destroyer fought its way through the high waves.

Confound it, the *Bismarck* must shoot now! They must have spotted us long ago. What's happened to the 15-inch shells? What has happened to the flashes from the muzzles, the impact, the splinters? Why are we approaching still closer? Hell, this was tempting Fate!

Five thousand yards, 4,800, 4,600... Where are the others? Where are *Sikh*, *Maori*, *Cossack* and Poirun? Why aren't they attacking from the other side? Are they making for the *Bismarck* at all?

'Torpedoes ready!'

As close as possible, thought Commander Graham. For safety's sake he ought to have zig-zagged, but the straightest way to the enemy was the quickest. He had long ago come within firing range, but the nearer he got to the *Bismarck* the more accurately he could aim his torpedoes. He would go on till the battleship fired the first salvo at him. Then he would release his eels in quick succession, one, two, three, four, and turn off.

The *Zulu* no longer had any radar. It had been shot to pieces an hour ago by a shell from the *Bismarck* fired at a range of 7,000 yards. One killed, two wounded. On the tween-deck, below the bridge, lay a bundle wrapped in grey blankets round which the crew stepped gingerly – Petty Officer Kingsly, who exactly sixty-one minutes ago had still been alive.

How many Kingslys would there be on board? How long would the destroyer hold to this crazy assault? Would *Zulu* blow up at the first salvo? Were the Germans asleep over there? For God's sake fire!

Range 4,500 yards. A star shell rent the darkness. It was fired by a destroyer and exploded close by the *Bismarck*, lighting up the ghostly scene in a sudden flash.

'Sir,' reported the Torpedo Officer, 'range favourable. Target sighted.'

'Take your time,' ordered the Commander. 'Keep steady. We shall wait for the enemy's first salvo. It won't be long. Easy does it.'

At this moment the *Bismarck* struck. There was a flash – the muzzle of her guns. Then something droned through the night. Heavy shells whined towards them. Straddle.

'Torpedoes fired,' reported the British officer.

Immediately the *Zulu* turned sharply away. Heeling heavily, she strove to right herself. Breakers poured over the deck. Shells landed to port and starboard, fore and aft.

How far can they follow us? Will they give up? They have to save their ammunition! Where are the others? Why don't they attack? And what about our torpedoes? Was it in vain, all that fear and courage?

'Probably no hit,' Commander Graham entered in the log.

He had two more torpedoes. He must approach the enemy again to fire them off.

The *Bismarck* had ceased to fire. Graham turned towards the enemy again, slowed down, as though to give the crew and the engines a breather. Perhaps the the others would bring it off. They themselves had achieved nothing, but they had got away safely once again.

What would happen next time?

Shells cracked again. They were no longer aimed at the *Zulu*. The *Bismarck* had trained her guns on another British destroyer. Suddenly there was a blinding flash. Hallucination? Or a hit on the *Bismarck*?

Or on one of the destroyers?

It was 3 a.m. and the night showed no sign of drawing to an end. Until it was swallowed up by day the five destroyers – or were there only four of them now? – must attack the *Bismarck* again and again. The quick, bold, almost suicidal decision of Captain Vian – who was just taking the *Cossack* as close as possible to the German flagship – had been expressly approved by Sir John Tovey, the British Commander-in-Chief.

By morning the British fleet's advance to the last decisive battle would be complete. Till then the destroyers were to allow the *Bismarck* no peace, they were to maintain contact, attack her, torpedo her, and, when they had fired their last torpedo, mark the *Bismarck*'s position with star shells. And the shells continued to whine...

Oppression, fear, dread, the *Bismarck*'s invisible escorts, slowly disappeared.

Fatalism took possession of the ship. Then came the turn to optimism. Almost suddenly. Men heard what they wanted to hear, all at once they believed what they were told and laughed at their gloomy thoughts. Cigarettes began to taste good once more. What was a No Smoking order? Nobody took it seriously any longer.

Out of the mass there arose nameless individuals, a few minutes ago unknown, who carried the others along with their *sang-froid*, their pluck, their confidence. Such men were present in every quarter of the ship, among all ranks. In a twinkling they had confederates, allies, imitators. Destiny could not be altered, but the frame of mind in which it was faced could be. For the time being, anyhow....

During the breathing spaces in the battle they relayed music from the wireless cabin. For a moment the men stared at the loudspeaker incredulously.

'*Warum ist es am Rhein so schön?* – Why is it so lovely by the Rhine?' asked a baritone.

There was laughter once more. Then the record fell silent.

'Enemy destroyer attack beaten off.'

So much for the Tommies. They must be crazy.

Ha, the old *Bismarck* was not dead yet, she was still shooting, still hitting the mark.

Another alarm. Destroyers.

Let them come! The radar scanner revealed their every movement. Permission to fire! Let them come closer. There was no risk. Even if their torpedoes struck, they would explode harmlessly against the armour plating. The only vulnerable point, the steering gear, was already smashed.

Commander Schneider, who an hour and a half ago had been awarded the Knight's Cross, the First Gunnery Officer, was authorized to act on his own initiative.

Take your time. Save ammunition. Few salvoes, but accurate. One destroyer lay ahead. Range about three miles. Any minute now she would be in the right spot. There was nothing to be seen. But radar is keener than the human eye. Marvellous invention!

Range 26 hundred, 24 hundred...

Now! The first salvo. Dead on target. But they noticed that on the other side.

Torpedoes away.

How can the enemy aim in such a sea? At that range? The torpedoes passed a long way off.

The destroyer turned away. Another salvo. Enough.

Star shells. All right, let them make light if they want to.

Then the second destroyer raced towards them. How many of the things had the British? And how many would they have in half an hour? Who could tell in this nocturnal chaos?

Discharge. Impact. Discharge. Impact.

A glow on the horizon. For a few seconds only. A hit? An explosion? It could do no harm to assume so. A few seconds later the loudspeaker announced:

'Enemy destroyer believed destroyed.'

This boosted morale. Which of the 2,402 men facing the last hours of their lives knew that the glow had also fooled the enemy? That aboard the *Zulu* they imagined the *Bismarck* had been hit and raised three cheers? On the *Zulu*, too, it was thought that a boost to morale would do no harm.

Commander Graham had the announcement made over the loudspeakers:

'*Bismarck* believed hit.'

That made two false reports – one German, the other British. On both sides hope was the father. Hope is international. It is the fighting-man's 'inner armour', whatever uniform he wears.

The destroyers sheered off. They came back. They fired at close quarters, then from further away – but they shot wide. They reported '*Bismarck* hit', but they failed to hit her. At about 3.30 a.m. there was a pause in the fighting. The destroyers gathered for a fresh assault.

Meanwhile a fresh record was put on in the *Bismarck*'s wireless cabin, cigarettes were lit, men talked and wrote. In a trice the rumour spread that work was still proceeding on the steering gear, that the screws were not damaged, that there was a prospect of steering the ship with the screws.

That meant escape.

Escape from the closing circle of overwhelming forces. The rumour was not denied. Captain Lindemann decided to tell a merciful lie:

'Attention! Attention!' came the announcement.

'Sixty-six Junker 88s have just taken off from Western France to attack the English fleet.'

'Did you hear that?' Pfeiffer said to Lauchs. 'Did you hear that? What did I tell you? Our bombers won't leave us in the lurch. I saw that once in the North Sea. There was a bang, and the ship was gone.'

'It's a guard of honour for your marriage by proxy,' commented Lauchs, turning to Link. 'They know what's expected of them.'

'But suppose they can't find us?' asked Pollack. 'Or don't hit their targets?'

'Don't work yourself up, chum,' Lauchs called out to him. 'It's lovely weather for bathing today, just the right temperature, nice waves.... Bloody hell, who swiped my booze?'

Moessmer was eating pineapple again. The third tin. The last in his life...

'Man,' he said, 'the lilac is in blossom now round my home.'

'So what?'

'Round mine, too,' Hengst broke in.

'Paint it on the wall,' retorted Lauchs laughing, 'complete with the scent.'

'This time I'm going to bring it off,' went on Lauchs. 'This leave I'll do it. You remember that red-headed bitch, Annemie, I told you about? I've been after her for two years. I'd just about got there. Then some lousy sergeant in the tanks came along. But he won't be around now. You've got to have luck. Don't worry. This time Annemie's for it.'

'Unless someone else snaps her up again.'

'I'd have to be stupid to let that happen.'

'You're stupid all right,' retorted Pfeiffer. 'But don't let it worry you, there are others even stupider.'

'Man, it's lucky for you I'm in a good mood.'

So it went on. The next twenty minutes passed quickly. Words stifled thoughts. The tongue is often in better shape than the head – at least during the last few hours before the holocaust.

People die in books and on the films. It's always other people who die. You can die in bed. But there's plenty of time for that. When you're seventy or eighty, or if possible even later. Nice and warm and cosy, as it should be. It's not so bad then. It has to come one day. But, man, that's forty or fifty years away. And we would like to live those years in peace and comfort. To work a bit, get on in life, have children and see them make good. Build a house, tend a garden. And a car, of course. And then go south for the holidays.

Wine, women and song, and spaghetti! This bloody war is bound to be over one day!

The officers, of course, knew how desperate, how hopeless the *Bismarck*'s position was. But they fed optimism with optimism. The Chief Engineer, for example, Commander Lehmann, whom the crew of the *Bismarck* affectionately called 'Daddy', was calmness personified. He smoked a cigar as he made his rounds, then he returned to his post and pressed his cigar into the hand of his messenger. Leading Artificer Springborn of X Half-Division.

'Hold that for a moment.'

Ten minutes later he came back. The messenger handed him the cigar. It had meanwhile gone out.

'Laddie, are you crazy? They cost 70 pfennig each. How can anyone let a cigar go out!'

The officer lit a second. In the course of his inspection he had to go into the engine-room. Again he handed his cigar to Springborn.

The messenger stood by the hatch smoking. A petty officer caught him at it.

'Didn't anyone ever tell you there's No Smoking?'

'I'm smoking on the orders of the Chief Engineer. You can ask him if you like, he's in there.'

Twenty minutes later the Commander squeezed himself through the hatch. With a grin, Springborn handed him the cigar, which he had smoked to a stub.

Lehmann laughed.

'You're learning quickly, my boy.'

That is called leadership...

Just then, at about 3.50 a.m. on this fatal day of 27 May, 1941, two young officers reported to the Captain, Lieutenant Richter and Sub-Lieutenant von Reisach.

'What is it, gentlemen?' asked Lindemann.

'Attempts to repair the steering gear have been abandoned, haven't they, sir?'

'You know they have.'

'We should like to volunteer for one last try. We have done diver training. We want to blow the rudder free from below.'

'How do you think you can get down in this sea?'

'It's worth trying, sir.'

'What good do you think it will do?'

'Attempts to blow it free from above failed. The only chance is to blow it free from underneath.'

'But you know very well you can't get down there.'

'Sir,' continued Lieutenant Richter, 'perhaps it would be possible for a diver to get down if he didn't worry about coming up again. It would have to be done very fast – straight down, attach the charge and release the fuse at once.'

Each of the three officers was thinking the same. Each of them knew about the hours of desperate attempts. Each of them knew what had gone on around the steering gear, how the ship had been almost hove to, how oil had been poured on the sea to calm it and how men in heavy suits had been lowered, only to be hauled up unconscious a few seconds later, never having got near their objective. Diving was impossible in this rough sea, Besides, one of the screws was probably damaged as well. Even if they succeeded in blowing free the jammed rudder, there was no guarantee that the ship could be steered with the screws.

The Captain knew what the two officers had in mind. They wanted to go down, weighted with ballast, knowing they would never come up again. They intended to attach the charge under water and blow themselves to pieces with it.

'I can't accept this sacrifice,' said Captain Lindemann, breaking the silence. 'I consider it pointless. Everything possible has already been tried.'

'But not what we are suggesting,' insisted Richter.

'Your courage does you honour,' replied Lindemann. 'You will have need of it later on today.'

'It would be better for two to die than for the whole ship to perish.'

'Be sensible, Richter. Why should you sacrifice yourself to no purpose? If I thought there was a chance.... Believe me, there's no point in trying. But thank you.'

My men, thought the Captain. Men of my school. Men who are ready to die for others. A lesson they learnt at the Staff College and put into practice on the *Bismarck*.

The Captain was pale and exhausted. But he looked calm and controlled. His unspoken confidence, his contempt for death radiated to those around him, spread to the whole ship. My God, mused the Captain, to think that men like that must die!

Then the destroyer attacked again.

In every part of the ship the will to live battled with the fear of death. Till the very moment of final destruction the *Bismarck* made desperate attempts to save herself. Now that the colossus had been shot into helplessness, the precision of her design and the excellence of her construction really became evident.

Because of the destroyers' almost incessant attacks, the bulkheads had been closed all night long. In the boiler-rooms, especially, the atmosphere had become intolerable. Men in leather clothing toiled in no degrees of heat and renounced their right to go off watch. One after the other was dragged off unconscious, but a few minutes later, as soon as they came round again, they were back, striving to get the last ounce out of the engines. The latter were switched straight over from 'full speed ahead' to 'full speed astern'. The ahead-valve was no sooner closed than the astern-valve was whipped open. It was amazing what a strain those engines stood up to.

The engine-room personnel had stuck slices of lemon between their dry, cracked lips. The protective clothing chafed their sweaty skin. The men were fighting with the last drop of energy against unconsciousness, against the heat, against the stench, against their nerves – against death.

Suddenly it had to be reported to the engine-room control position that one of the turbines was no longer turning with the rest.

'Give it everything you've got,' came the order.

'Steam up. Kill or cure!' shouted a Leading Artificer.

Four hundred and thirty, 570, 830. One valve was open to place the load on the wheels of one side of the turbines only. At 830 lb. per square inch steam pressure, at 750° F. and with the safety valves shut tight! More steam still!

At last the second valve received pressure. Thirty, 60, 90, 200 atmospheres.

Horror-struck, the men watched this frightful experiment for which, under normal circumstances, the Chief Engineer would have been court-martialled.

Then the engine sprang to life. Without a fracture. Without smashed blades. The final triumph of German shipbuilding... Too late. As the ship went down, shattered by gunfire, a bare ten hours later, the turbine went on turning.

The last hours before the battle weighed heaviest on the men who had nothing to do – the civilian stewards, who were now trotting round with red-cross arm-bands, the men of the boarding parties, the aircrews, the craftsmen in the tailors' and shoemakers' work-shops.

One unoccupied member of the crew was Lieutenant-Commander Nobis, who had been put out of work by the torpedo that smashed the *Bismarck*'s rudder. He stared at the chart... and marked the position at which the German flagship would be intercepted and sunk. A tiny, dark blue dot made with an indelible pencil, like the full-stop at the end of a sentence. But here it marked the end of more than a sentence.

If only the next few hours were already over. If only there were no thoughts, no memories, none of this balancing of accounts, this lotting up of things not done. Fear of the end had been tormenting him for so long that Nobis imagined he no longer felt it. He had got used to it and he hoped that when the last hour came he would behave as he had resolved to behave. That he would die as he ought. That he would not be weaker than those whose fate he shared....

How long was it since he was celebrated in his Silesian home as a hero before he became one? Since he was put on show, since absurdly inflated articles were written about him in the local paper? Since he was photographed on display at a brownshirt rally! He didn't feel at home among these people. It was purely a question of feeling. He had scarcely thought about them. Politics didn't interest him. Not then... but now, as he went to his death... What for? Now it was too late...

He spoke to nobody about Deina. His father had once surprised him looking at her photograph.

'Who is that?' asked the old man.

'A girl.' He was about to put the photograph away, but Father Nobis took it, as though as a matter of course, and looked at it.

'A pretty girl... where does she live?'

'In Portugal.'

'Fancy that,' commented his father. 'Tell me about her.'

'There's nothing to tell.'

'Are you in love with her?'

The young officer became gruff.

'I'm in love with her,' he said reluctantly, 'but the devil take me for it.'

In the evening his father spoke of her again. He'put the newspaper aside.

'There's one thing I don't understand, my boy,' he began out of the blue. 'Why didn't you stay with her?'

'Could I have done?'

'Everyone must know what he can do... I'm older than you. Perhaps you were right. But probably I'm right... I'm your father. Fathers are egoistic in these things. It's enough for me that my eldest son died in Poland.'

'We misunderstand one another,' objected Werner Nobis. 'It was precisely because Hans died in Poland that I came back.'

'Well,' said his father, closing the conversation, 'I would rather you hadn't come back till *after* the war.'

How right he was! He would soon be entirely alone. He, too, would soon remember that conversation. And his despair would last longer than his son's, who would have got it over in a few hours.

Deina! God God, how close she was. How she stood before him, almost within reach. How clearly he could see her as she talked to him directly after they first met.

'I hate the war,' she said. 'It is murdermg the best. On both sides. For a puffed-up nonentity. We could go swimming now or play tennis. Wouldn't you like to?'

"Of course I should like to."

'Can't you imagine loving something more than the war?'

'I don't love war. I'm merely doing my duty.'

'A wonderful duty,' she retorted, 'shooting other people dead and being shot dead yourself. God, it's really none of my business. Perhaps you will think differently one day. Perhaps a day will come when you will love something more deeply than your duty. A woman, for example.'

'I'm within an ace of it already,' replied Nobis. It sounded stupid and empty.

Today he would no longer have said it. But today he couldn't say anything any more. It was all over.

Done for. Ruined. Thrown away. If he could only have told her, just once, how much he regretted everything. How differently he would act next time... But there wasn't going to be a next time.

Dawn broke. On the British side the situation was quite clear. The destroyers were still keeping the *Bismarck* occupied. They had long since used up their torpedoes. The last to run in close to the enemy was Captain Vian's *Cossack*. That she once more escaped the concentric fire of the 15-inch guns was almost a miracle. In the grey morning light Captain Vian placed his destroyers in a wide square round the *Bismarck*. They had come out of the night's action unscathed, save for a hit on the *Zulu*. Both sides had observed a gigantic flash that remains to this day unexplained.

Aboard *Ark Royal* the planes were preparing to take off and shadow the enemy. Astern of the British flagship, *King George V*, lay the *Rodney*. She had orders to follow the flagship's movements only in general direction. The over-rigid battle formation of the British units during the *Hood* engagement had proved disastrous. Admiral Tovey knew only the approximate position of the *Bismarck*. But he was lucky. At 8.15 a.m. the *Norfolk*, which was crossing the area of operations, sighted at a distance of 8 sea miles a battleship which she took to be the *Rodney*. At the last moment she realized it was the *Bismarck*, towards which she was steaming at a rate of 20 knots. The *Norfolk* hauled sharply away and reported the *Bismarck*'s course to Admiral Tovey. The Admiral steered towards her. To within a distance of 8 miles. He had only to wait.

So far so good. But he was worried about oil. If the *Bismarck* was not destroyed by midday at the latest Tovey would have to break off the engagement, otherwise his ship would never make port. As it was, five hours before this maximum period, it was doubtful whether all the British vessels were still capable of doing so. If German aircraft appeared on the scene! If German U-boats arrived! If they had to steer a zig-zag course at full speed and so increase oil consump-tion by several hundred per cent! There was only one solution – to bring the *Bismarck* to battle and destroy her at once.

Shortly before the enemy's final assault Admiral Lütjens decided to have the *Bismarck*'s log brought to safety in France by the ship's planes. Of the five Arado 196s, which the flagship carried, three were still airworthy. The other two had been damaged by blast during a torpedo attack.

The aircrew had asked again and again for leave to go into action. They wanted to act as fighters against the Swordfish. But Admiral Lütjens insisted on keeping the Arados in safety. He felt they had no chance, because of the numerical superiority of the British planes. He wished to preserve them, as he thought, for more important purposes.

Now came the order to make the three operational machines ready for take-off. The crews were ordered to report to the First Officer. 'We shall slow down. The log will be stowed in the first machine. Best of luck.'

Clad in fur-lined flying suits, Flight-Lieutenant Friedrich and Warrant-Officer Schniewind watched the preparation of the catapult. Take-off conditions were bad.

It was still dark. Enemy fighters had no chance yet. From every side men rushed up to the two airmen and pressed notes and letters into their hands – poignant, scribbled farewells to parents, wives and children.

'All set,' reported an artificer.

'The rats are leaving the sinking ship,' grumbled a petty officer.

'Shut your trap,' retorted another.

'Do you think they'll get through?'

"They've got more chance than we have, anyway.'

'That's not difficult.'

'Next war I'll volunteer for the *Luftwaffe*... As long as everything's cushy, they play skat, and when things hot up they beat it.'

The men on the upper deck watched spellbound as Flight-Lieutenant Friedrich and Warrant-officer Schniewind climbed into the first machine. The seamen's gaze hung like lead upon this bird about to soar. How many of them wished they could cling to the plane. They all wanted to get out of this floating mouse-trap, this ship condemned to destruction. As they stood there they suddenly felt alone, although not more than six men at most were about to fly away.

If everything went according to plan...

The propeller had been swung, the engine warmed up. In a moment they would be off. The Flight-Lieutenant at the joy-stick nodded. The catapult artificer saw the signal.

Now the first Arado would be shot from the deck by compressed air...

With a violent movement Flight-Lieutenant Karl-Heinz Friedrich shook off his feeling of numbness. He saw the staring, burning eyes of those who were being left behind, and for a moment he felt almost em-barrassed because he would be saved. He sat behind the Arado's joy-stick, in his own kingdom, his own world.

He primed the engine. It whined into life, the air-screw turned at such speed that the men in the plane had to hold tight to avoid being blown over.

Brakes off. Test the tail plane. The rudder control. A glance at the rev meter. The fuel gauge. The oil pressure gauge. The altimeter. The electric circuits.

Everything okay.

Ready for catapulting off. Away from the damned ship, up into the air. On a homing course. In a matter of hours all this would be three hundred miles behind him. These cursed seven days that hung from his nerves like leaden weights.

The air-crews had had nothing to do. Nothing at all. They only had to wait. For the order to take off that never came. Always ready. Day and night in their flying kit. On the flight deck when the shells came whistling over, when the air-raid warning sounded, when the ship's crew were at action stations, each one at his post, at his lever, at his task. They were ridiculed and envied 'holidaymakers', condemned to play skat while the others fought.

It was beyond endurance.

They were forced to watch as miserable Swordfish torpedoed the *Bismarck*, as enemy spotter planes circled in the air over the German flagship. What a fate for a *Luftwaffe* pilot to be seconded to a warship!

Two days ago Flight-Lieutenant Karl-Heinz Friedrich had reported to the Captain.

'Sir, I request permission to take off.'

'Why, Friedrich?'

'It would be an easy job to shoot down that Catalina.'

'Then another one would come along.'

'I'd shoot that down as well.'

Lindemann smiled.

'It's not so simple,' he, said benevolently. 'It takes us twenty minutes to get you up. We should have to re-duce speed... Do you know what that means? And what guarantee have I that you wouldn't be shot down?... Your turn will come, Flight-Lieutenant.'

'I was a fighter pilot, sir.'

'I know,' replied the Captain. 'And I value the fact, Flight-Lieutenant. I haven't forgotten you.'

Only when he was back with his comrades did Friedrich remember all the things he had intended to say in reporting to the Commander. Damn it all, what were Catalina's and Swordfish! He had shot down four Spitfires over France! He was awarded the Iron Cross when most of his squadron never got back. What was a Catalina compared with a Spitfire!

Again they had to wait. Again they had to put up with the torment of being on board ship. Again in action gnawed insidiously at their morale.

The Flight-Lieutenant was a vigorous young officer of the sort the times produced. He was born with a silver spoon in his mouth. The only son of a bank director, who glanced through his school reports and then prescribed a spot of private tuition. This saw him through into the next class. The best in his class at boxing and swimming, on the horizontal bar and the parallel bars. A Hitler Youth leader, of course – field games, nights under canvas and evenings round the camp fire to the accompaniment of patriotic songs and burning words taken with all the bitter seriousness of youth.

Then came gliding, just the sport for Karl-Heinz Friedrich. How fast he learnt, how quickly he became familar with wind, sun and air currents. With what ease he passed his tests and gained his A, B and C Certificates. He wore the white wings on a blue ground with the same pride as veterans of World War I wore their Iron Crosses on ex-servicemen's parades.

Then came the school-leaving certificate. Once more luck was on his side, for war had already broken out and it cared nothing for a B in Latin and an even worse D in maths. He was called up to the *Luftwaffe*. Shot down twice while still a Pilot Officer. Extra quick promotion to Flight-Lieutenant. Shot down for the fourth time on his twentieth birthday. Immediately after this landed with a burning plane, dragged free of the wreckage. Sewn up in hospital. Convalescent leave.

Then the business with Ortrud was settled. They had been neighbours and played together, until it became too unmanly for Karl-Heinz to play with a girl. She was just out of finishing-school when he met her again. He made straight at her in the manner of a fighter pilot and she was instantly aflame. Youth brooks no delay, especially in wartime. They found one another before they were betrothed. They intended to go through the formalities later, when they had time – in a few days perhaps, if everything went off all right. Devil take it, why shouldn't everything go off all right?

Flight-Lieutenant Friedrich had his hand on the joy-stick and was thinking of Ortrud. Be careful at the take-off! Don't crash! Rubbish, of course he wouldn't crash.

He had 400 miles to fly. The Arado had a range of 750 miles. Everything was ready. A last wave to the catapult crew. Throttle open. The lever was pushed down...

'Damnation, what's wrong?'

The catapult had failed. They'd have to get out.

'Bloody hell,' swore Warrant-Officer Schniewind.

Friedrich stopped the engine and climbed out of the plane.

'There's nothing to get excited about,' called the artificer. 'The compressed air pipe is bent. We'll soon put that right.'

The Flight-Lieutenant nodded. Damn it, why didn't they notice that before? he thought bitterly. Well, the main thing was to get off eventually. Another cigarette. Another chat with the crews of the two planes waiting to take off after him. A few more notes with messages to relations. A few more despairing jokes by those who had to stay behind.

'Ready!' called the artificer.

Friedrich and Schniewind climbed into their bird. Throttle open. Catapult lever down.

Again nothing happened.

Another try.

In vain.

'Come out,' shouted the engineer officer. 'You can't take off. The guide rail is smashed. The torpedo must have done it.'

'What does that mean?'

'There's nothing we can do about it.'

Friedrich got a grip on himself. No one must see how he felt. Come on, laugh! His voice mustn't shake.

He mustn't stumble. Damn it, he mustn't tremble. Come on, a joke!

'Well,' he said to Schniewind, so loudly that the bystanders couldn't fail to hear. 'Now we're proper holidaymakers, we'll be going for a bathe.'

'All right, I can swim,' replied the Warrant-Officer.

Back on his deck Friedrich threw the pile of notes and letters on the locker. That's that, he thought.

'It makes me sick,' said Schniewind.

'Be sick, if you want to!'

A horrible indifference came over the raw young officer. He suddenly felt that none of it mattered to him any more, as though he was watching his own fate with cool interest through opera glasses from a box at the theatre. Fear had beaten a retreat, a spirit of utter indifference gradually took possession of him and lay like a merciful veil over his thoughts and hopes, over his fate.

'So we shan't be playing postman after all.' Flight-Lieutenant Friedrich picked up one of the notes lying in front of him and read it out.

My dear Parents,

At this hour, which may be one of my last, I am thinking of you, I am with you, I embrace you. Perhaps we shall be together again and put this letter on the fire laughing. But if things work out differently, please bear it with the same courage with which I must bear it. Now, at this hour, I want to believe that we shall meet after death. I cling to this belief. Good luck.

Your Erich.

'It's like a message on a funeral wreath,' added the Flight-Lieutenant.

'It'll be a first-class funeral,' replied Warrant-Officer Schniewind.

'Yes.' The Flight-Lieutenant lit a cigarette. He watched to see whether his hand was trembling. 'I don't think dying is so bad,' he said then.

'At least you haven't a wife and children,' answered Schniewind.

I've got Ortrud, thought the Flight-Lieutenant, and parents. Who hasn't and who isn't thinking of them?

Some hours later Flight-Lieutenant Karl-Heinz Friedrich set an example of how to die with calm fortitude, standing on the upper deck at exactly the spot from which he should have taken off for his homeward flight.

By then there was nothing much left of the battleship *Bismarck*. Her upper works were in shreds, her last shell fired. Hundreds of her crew were already dead. The wounded were trying to drag themselves along the deck to the sick-bay. Full up. No entry. The whole ship had become a sick-bay.

The Admiral was dead. The cutter and the lifeboats destroyed. The rafts shattered. Life-jackets inflated. The ship was ready to be blown up. Wherever you looked, there was blood, corpses, men torn to shreds, gasping, screaming, beseeching, dying.

Mountainous waves crashed against the ship's sides. 'Every man for himself!' But what hope was there for any of them?

In their terror the first to go overboard jumped the wrong side. The waves hurled them against the ship, smashing in their skulls. Somewhere in the background was the enemy. He had temporarily ceased fire. Between the enemy and the *Bismarck* drifted puddles of oil.

'We've got to get through that,' said Schniewind.

'It'll gum up the pores of our skin. And we shall suffocate. To hell with it all! To hell with this damned Navy! I knew right away it would turn out badly. I'm not leaving the ship.'

'What are you going to do?'

The young man, one of millions the war had swallowed, digested and spat out, had made up his mind. He stood there calm and pale. He had seen it all on the films and discussed it round the camp fire. He had believed in it, and it had filled him with enthusiasm. There was no enthusiasm left now.

It was all over in a flash.

He whipped out his revolver. The Warrant-Officer tried to knock it out of his hand.

'Stand back!' The Flight-Lieutenant roared at him. He put it to his temple. Was such a thing really possible? Wasn't this like the cheapest sort of film? Wasn't it madness? Wasn't it utterly stupid?

'Long live the Führer and Great Germany!' cried Karl-Heinz Friedrich. Then the shot rang out...

One more death aboard the *Bismarck*. The number had long since ceased to count. There was an inflation in heroic deaths. Three members of the air-crews followed their Flight-Lieutenant's example. Only they managed without his last dramatic declaration.

They died without a word...

Another five hours were to pass before Flight-Lieutenant Friedrich and his comrades reached that point. It was now 5 a.m. and the day had a long way to go. It was deep grey everywhere. On this 27 May, the light was hesitatingly breaching the first gaps in the wall of grey-black cloud.

At this point Admiral Sir John Tovey revised his decision to bring the *Bismarck* to bay at first light. Because of the bad visibility and in spite of his acute fuel shortage he let another two hours pass. It seemed to him that in the dim light there was too much risk of one of his own ships being mistaken for the enemy.

Reports from the destroyers were continually reaching the British flagship *King George V*. The crews of the British warships had spent the whole night at action stations. Then they were allowed to stand down and sleep in shifts. Now, immediately before the final clash, they were fed with benzedrine tablets and pep talks. Rumour was even swifter than the official loudspeaker announcements, which repeatedly referred to the severe damage suffered by the *Bismarck*.

The outlines of *King George V* and *Rodney* emerged hesitantly from the darkness, and the mighty 16-inch guns came up over the horizon. Slowly, infinitely slowly, daylight pierced the gloom as the hands of the clock moved round. Chaplains went through the ship saying prayers. Letters were written, jokes made, stories told, the future discussed, tea poured out, with a shot of rum this time and a double ration of sugar. Fear was repressed and the certainty of victory disseminated.

As he went down the ladder from the Admiral's bridge, an officer came upon a number of rats scurrying about in terror. He swallowed his fright and said nothing. Sailors are superstitious...

The *Ark Royal*'s Swordfish took off almost vertically into the wind. They were to shadow the *Bismarck*. A further torpedo attack from the air was postponed. The battle was to be fought in broad daylight.

Every now and then the men on the *Bismarck* would stop and listen for the promised Junkers 88 dive-bombers. They ought to have been there long ago, they ought to be launching their relieving attack and breaking the phalanx of the overwhelmingly powerful enemy.

One after the other they gave up their last hope, clutched at it again, rejected it, resigned themselves afresh, cursed, prayed, kept silent, listened, wrote, whispered, blustered. One after the other they looked at the time, enquired about German U-boats, thought of their homes, ate, smoked, grappled with their terror.

'Hey, chum,' Able Seaman Lauchs called out to his shipmate Pfeiffer, 'what's happened to your Stukas?'

'The fellows must still be sitting in the latrines... Ask Hengst, he always knows everything.'

'They're bound to come over sooner or later,' broke in Link.

'There's more likelihood of the Admiral running around the deck naked than of those planes turning up.'

'That's a nice idea,' roared Moessmer, 'tell him to get cracking.'

'Don't kid yourselves, chum. The game's up,' rejoined Lauchs.

The same moment, he too stood still and listened to the sound of imaginary aeroplanes.

'Don't strain your ears,' said Pollack. 'That was Moessmer.'

'Shut your trap,' the latter snapped at him.

'How far is it to France?' asked Link.

"They could manage it with auxiliary tanks.'

'Then they'll come,' asserted Link.

'When it's too late... Those *Luftwaffe* fellows like to have it cushy,' stated Lauchs. 'The weather isn't good enough for them.'

'Shut up, will you!' yelled Pollack. 'You're just driving each other nuts. If you can't help being in a blue funk, at least keep quiet about it.'

'If only there were a few U-boats about!'

All of a sudden the whole ship started.

A song put a stop to conversation – the *Bismarck*'s melody of Fate.

'Come back.'

Everyone's hope was all at once expressed in this song. Suddenly everyone stared at the loudspeaker.

Everyone imagined he could see in front of him the embodied wishes of his family, their faces, their anxious waiting. Suddenly they all felt they were no longer alone. Only a few days ago the announcer had said at the end of the

Request Concert:

'Now we have a request that comes from the whole German nation, a request for the gallant crew of the *Bismarck*: "Come back".'

At that moment a thrill had run through everyone.

But how much had happened between that day and this, between the intoxication of victory following the sinking of the *Hood* and the foreknowledge of their own doom!

'Come back', a song that would be played today as every day in the cafés, whose words were sung in German, French and Italian, whose tune loving couples gaily hummed and to whose rhythm school-boys practised their first stiff foxtrot steps.

This Tin Pin Alley melody carried away a whole ship, 2,402 destinies, deadened fear, lifted up those in despair and gave them a straw to cling to during the final hours when there was nothing else left to cling to. As though moved by a ghostly hand the needle was continually moved back, the record continued playing until it went down with the ship...

> '*Come back to me,*
> *I'm waiting for you,*
> *Since I first saw you*
> *You've been all to me.*'

The men listened with ardour, with conviction, with enchantment. They murmured the words as though they were a prayer that would render them immune from hell.

> '*No matter how long*
> *The road may be*
> *It will lead us both*
> *To ecstasy.*
> *So hear my song,*
> *Come back to me.*'

The upper works would fly apart, gun turrets be smashed to pieces, decks burn, oil tanks blow up, orders come thick and fast, men die by the hundred – but the record went on turning. Men went to their death with its notes still ringing in their ears...

At 7 a.m. the *Bismarck* sent out her last radio message:

'Send U-boat to save ship's log. Fleet Commander.'

The *Bismarck* was making straight for the enemy.

Her radar scanner had long ago picked up the hostile ships. But because she was impossible to manoeuvre she was compelled to leave the initiative to the British. She had to wait while the enemy placed himself in a good firing position. The last alarm was sounded. All hands to action stations!

This was the time of day when people at home fetched the newspaper from the letter-box, read it from back to front, because the announcements of deaths were the most important features, swallowed a wretched breakfast and tried to meet the postman before standing in a queue for some special issue on the ration cards. The children were at school as usual. Over the radio came the latest news from Crete. Leading articles were still devoted to the *Bismarck*'s victory over the *Hood*. So the families of the 2,402 men of the *Bismarck* knew that their husbands and sons were in action.

Able Seaman Pollack's wife had given birth two days before to a seven-pound boy. There were complications, but mother and child were now doing fine.

Sub-Lieutenant Peters's mother was writing a letter.

Frau Burger had just learnt that her son had undergone an operation for appendicitis on board the *Bismarck*. A last letter written in Bergen had reached her by a roundabout route.

Else Birken was getting ready for her proxy wedding. Her appointment was for ten o'clock. She had had a navy blue costume made from material she had hoarded up, and she looked nice in it. At the registry office the chair beside her would be symbolically empty. She had to put on her own ring. It was only a ceremony, but from excitement the girl was ready two and a half hours before the wedding. The armament factory had given her the day off. Her father would go with her to the registry office.

There were relatives of the men of the *Bismarck* all over Germany. They hoped for as long as they could. Many possessed the gift of keeping thought and worry at bay. Others thought day and night of their sons. They shared their fate with millions – a whole nation was waiting for post.

A young girl also waited who was not related to anyone on the *Bismarck*, who knew nothing at all about the *Bismarck*.

A girl in Portugal – Deina, who belonged to Lieutenant-Commander Werner Nobis, yet did not belong to him.

When Deina awoke that morning in Oporto, when her eyes sought Werner, she knew at once that he had gone, that he had run away from her, from their love, from his happiness, in order to get back into the war. She couldn't take it in. She raged. Resigned herself. And loved...

Deina was tough and strong-willed. The more she told herself she hated the German Lieutenant, the closer he seemed to be to her. She became aware of the powerlessness of her hate sooner than of the power of her love. Finally she noticed that she was angrier with herself than with Werner Nobis. She was all at sixes and sevens. When things came to such a pass, a young girl turns at last to her mother.

Her mother listened to Deina without interrupting her. She did not utter her reproaches; but this made them all the worse.

'What now?' she asked at last.

'I don't know what to do any more.'

The mother looked at her daughter closely. Deina didn't want to cry, and so she didn't cry. She looked young, fresh and pretty as on any other day. She knew how to keep her suffering out of sight.

'First you must make up your mind,' went on her mother, 'whether you really love the man.'

'I do.'

'What about him?'

'He loves me too.'

'Then I don't understand why he left you.'

Deina shrugged her shoulders. She was in the process of understanding it without being able to grasp it. Without approving of it. But somehow it impressed her in spite of everything; sometimes a foolish action is all part of a person's character.

'How do you know he loves you?' her mother continued.

'You feel a thing like that.'

'You can't always rely on your feelings.'

Deina now spoke a trifle louder and more vehemently, but there was a trace of resignation beneath her fervour.

'What can I rely on, if I can't trust my feelings any more?'

My God, thought her mother, what can I say to her, how can I help her? Why did she have to pick a damned German to fall in love with? Deina's mother had nothing against Germans. In fact all she knew about them was that they made good machines and bad wars.

'How can that go on?' she asked.

'I don't know,' replied Deina. 'I only know that it must go on. I'm only afraid he won't dare to come back, even if he can, that he will think I hate him for leaving me.'

'If he loves you he will come back,' her mother consoled her. She knew she was lying. But she also knew that at the moment this was the only consolation she had to offer.

Weeks and months passed. Lieutenant Werner Nobis was never again discussed between mother and daughter. But Deina thought of him continually. Through Portuguese friends she got in touch with the German consulate at Lisbon in an attempt to trace him. The consulate politely promised to help, but pointed to the complicated chain of enquiries that had to be made when asked for news of progress. Deina knew that Werner could only have escaped to Germany via Spain. So she asked the Spaniards for information. They wouldn't or couldn't tell her anything either.

So for a long time Deina heard nothing of Nobis. She thought of him and went on hoping, full of confidence, full of anxiety, full of anger. Full of love.

That he was an officer on board the German flagship *Bismarck* she did not know until much, much later.

At 8.43 a.m. the British units sighted the grey outline of a battleship 12 sea miles away.

'*Bismarck* in sight,' reported the lookout.

Admiral Sir John Tovey immediately gave permission to fire. His plans had been carefully worked out. Battle positions had been taken up. Four minutes later the British fired their first salvo. The *Rodney*'s 16-inch turrets flashed out. Twenty seconds later the *King George V* entered the engagement.

The *Bismarck* remained silent.

What was wrong? Why didn't she reply? Had her turrets broken down? Had she run out of ammunition? Did she want the enemy to approach closer still?

Doubt lasted only two minutes. Then there was a flash' on the opposite horizon.

'Fifty-five seconds flying time,' reported a British gunnery officer.

The wounded German giant turned her fire upon the *Rodney*. Her first salvo fell short. But her third was already straddling.

Rodney swung round to port and brought all her guns into play. *King George V* was still steaming straight at the enemy, firing as she went from all the guns of her forward turrets. Her fire was accurate. The first impact was observed. *Rodney* was zig-zag-ging to dodge the enemy's shells.

From the north-east the *Norfolk* was racing to join in the fight.

The sea looked as though it was on fire. Shell's fell hissing into the water. Ships were hit. There were flashes. Smoke. Wreckage. Splinters. Flames. Explosions.

Hell was lose.

The British advanced relentlessly towards the foe to deliver the death blow...

The time had come. It was only a matter of seconds before the first enemy shells landed. Only now did Admiral Lütjens give permission to fire. If only the ship was intact! If only he could zig-zag! If only the promised air support was available, if U-boats had come to his aid! If courage alone could defeat the enemy's manifold numerical superiority!

As it was, the *Bismarck* ploughed on, a defenceless target for the enemy guns. Her ammunition and her fuel both running low. She took her last desperate defensive action.

The British were shooting damned accurately. Guns fired, shells landed.

Hit to port, hit to starboard.

Hit to port again, then amidships.

Damage control parties went to work. There were screams. Contact between different parts of the ship was lost. There were clouds of smoke. The superstructure was in ruins.

One of the enemy's very first salvoes scored a direct hit on the Admiral's bridge. One of the first of the crew to die was Admiral Lütjens.

'Devil take Western Command!' he said a few seconds earlier.

But the fight to the death had only just begun. For two hours death rained down on the *Bismarck* from all sides. There was nothing left for the blazing, shattered, paralysed colossus to do but to show the way to die...

Faithful to death....

But this death, this gallant but senseless, wretched holocaust, wore a thousand masks. Men died in the bows, in the stern, on the bridge, on the lower deck, in the boiler-room. Each death was different. Some of them died slowly, a few of them quickly, sometimes mercifully, but more often pitilessly.

A handful of men death allowed to go free.

Perhaps destiny preserved them so that their accounts might be the most shattering of all testimonies against war...

The sky was darkened by the sulphur-yellow smoke from the shell-bursts. Day turned into night, and this night rent by dazzling flashes, by explosions at the gun mouth and explosions where the shells landed, became an artificial veil hiding the carnage.

For a split second explosions lit up the outlines of the inferno, marked for the space of a heartbeat the stations of the death that was swallowing up the young sailors by groups. One moment they were still standing at their posts, fighting, cursing, hoping, despairing or praying, but at the next salvo they lay torn in pieces or bleeding to death in the chaos of destruction.

The British gunners had found their range. Every shot was a hit, every hit a dozen heroic deaths. The *Bismarck*'s return fire had grown weak, spasmodic, in-accurate. 'A' turret fell silent. 'C' turret was answering with one gun only.

On the area of the upper deck known as 'Hindenburg Square' the dead were piled up in heaps. The upper works round the control mast were ablaze. Seamen shut in by the flames were screaming for help. The German flagship was turning into a wreck.

But the crew went on fighting. The Captain still stood on the bridge, cut off from his men by a wall of fire, linked with them by loudspeakers. His orders were still carried out as rapidly as possible. Discipline still snapped its fingers at death and destruction. A terrible, desperate courage still held the survivors together. Men still rose to the level of heroes, justifying by their deeds this hackneyed and misused word... till the last hour, the last minute, the last second. Those who could staggered to their feet, stumbled over dead and wounded, slipped on the scattered cartridges and reported at any assembly point they could find for a new job.

Number One fell. Number Two was seriously wounded. There wasn't any Number Three any more. The section officer was no longer alive. Section disbanded by death! New faces. New orders. New shells. New explosions.

War dropped its mask and for a few hours showed its sickening, murderous face, grinned at slogans, chewed up watchwords, scoffed at high-sounding phrases, played with men, hopes, dreams, broke up a crew of 2,402 into so many individual destinies...

At the beginning of the last battle Leading Seaman Bruno Rzonca was with Petty Officer Putsch and three men forming a damage control party in Compartment XII on the starboard side. The first hit landed on the port side. Five killed. Stinking smoke entered eyes and lungs. It stank of burning rubber and sulphur. Rzonca had forgotten his smoke mask.

'Stay at the telephone,' Petty Officer Putsch shouted to him, 'as long as you can stick it.'

Another hit.

Rzonca was the only survivor from his group. Terrible minutes passed before he realized this. Coughing, almost blind he pressed the telephone receiver to his ear. The rasping voice had fallen silent. What more could he do here?'

The direct hit had put him out of work. The Leading Seaman bent over one of his fallen shipmates. He stared at the contorted, burnt face, vomited, started to run away, forced himself to stand still, took off the man's smoke mask, saw the blood, threw it away, hurried forward and to the other side, reported to Compartment IX and was given a new job.

Immediately after this a group of radio operators raced across the tween-deck panic-stricken, stopped at a hatchway and began to climb.

'Stop!' Rzonca yelled at them. 'You must be crazy. Things are much worse up there.'

'Our cabin's on fire,' replied the foremost of the group laconically. 'We don't want to be burnt alive.'

'You'll be burnt still quicker up above.'

'I don't care,' shouted an Able Seaman, 'I'd rather die on deck. At least I shall be able to see what's going on.'

A shell landed near by. The paint caught fire. The stench was unbearable, the heat frightful.

Rzonca joined the radio operators and together they fought their way through to the aft dressing-station.

He stood horror-struck till a Surgeon-Lieutenant bellowed at him. Bedlam reigned. Men without arms, without legs were crying out hoarsely, begging for water, cigarettes, morphia, asking to be carried up on deck.

A Sick Berth Petty Officer pressed two ridiculous little packets of bandage into Rzonca's hand. Rzonca tore them open and bent over a wounded man.

'Take it easy, chum,' he said.

'Don't,' answered the man in a low voice. 'There's no sense. Go to the others. I'll have had my lot in a minute.'

Rzonca choked back nausea, fear and horror. He couldn't stand it here. He had to get out, out of the dressing-station. It was better to handle shells on the gunnery deck as long as it was still possible.

Another hit. Heavy stuff. The light went out. There were screams everywhere. Water poured in. The surviving surgeons and sick berth attendants went on bandaging in the darkness, up to their knees in water. To the right and left of them, behind and in front of them, wounded men were drowning with a gurgle, unable to hold their heads above the water that had poured in.

Another hit. Panic. All who had legs ran. Rzonca, too, made for the upper deck.

What would happen if the ship blew up? Dozens, hundreds were asking themselves the same question at this moment. Some two hundred men, the survivors of decimated teams like himself, were standing amidships at the ladder to the upper deck, trying to force the hatch open.

Suddenly there came an order. An officer. In a flash panic was stilled. Men marked by the fear of death stood one behind the other, waiting patiently while those in front opened the hatch.

It jammed. Suddenly all the hatches were jammed. They could flee no further than the gunnery deck. They came from the forecastle, from the bows. They were yelling, running, fleeing in pandemonium. The blast from bursting shells had bent the hatches. They fled on through the galleys. Everything was smashed up here too. There was a smell of wine and spirits. One man knelt down over a puddle of spirits on the floor and lapped up the alcohol. Two others stood there vomiting. Here the hatch budged two inches and then stuck.

Suddenly someone saw a hole. Daylight? Then dozens saw it; they pushed and shoved forwards, became jammed together and blocked the way to the supposed daylight. Those in front reached the spot. The next second the floor disappeared from under their feet and they fell down a blazing hole several yards deep. There were screams, the screams of dying men.

It was not a hatch. That had been a fatal illusion. It was the hole blown through the deck by a high-explosive shell to a paint store, that was now blazing. The onrushing men saw and heard nothing. Like those before them, they shot over the edge and down into the deadly mirage. At the last moment Rzonca saw what was in front of him. He threw himself to the ground and with his last ounce of strength thrust himself back inch by inch from the blazing abyss. Those behind tripped and stumbled over him as though blind. The Leading Seaman gripped one of them by the leg. But with a tremendous effort the man broke free and staggered into the flames. Rzonca yelled under the trampling sea boots. But everyone was yelling at that moment.

His body lost all feeling. More and more raced over him and tumbled down into the burning hole. Six feet from this gruesome sport of death, tramped upon, almost unconscious with horror, incapable of action, Leading Seaman Rzonca watched his shipmates burnt up before his eyes.

At last he managed to rise to his feet. He was able to hold back two or three men. One of them went to the edge of the crater and looked down.

'Don't look,' Rzonca told him dully.

'It's all over for them,' replied the man coolly. His face was green, his hands trembled, his eyes had a staring, crazed look. Perhaps I should have let myself be dragged down with the rest, thought Rzonca, then it would be all over for me too.

If only it wasn't for this atrocious fear. This impulse to save oneself even when there was no hope of salvation left.

No hope of salvation? The majority of the crew that were still alive struggled desperately against this thought. While there's a shred of life, there's hope...

Leading Seaman Rzonca, who had tasted death at sea in all its varied horror, had no idea that Fate would save him to bear witness against this mass murder unleashed.

He staggered numbly on....

As the battle proceeded, the British units drew closer and closer to the crippled German flagship. Twelve minutes after the start of the battle, *King George V* lay a bare 16,000 yards from *Bismarck*. Sir John Tovey veered on to a southerly course and so brought all his guns into play. *Rodney* observed his manoeuvre and followed suit. The two British battleships were no more than three sea miles apart. From further away the *Norfolk*, which was racing up from the north, Joined in the battle with her 8-inch guns.

Bismarck switched her fire from *Rodney* to *King George V*. But again it was inaccurate. One of the forward turrets was damaged. Through his glasses the *Rodney*'s First Gunnery Officer observed a hit on the main fire control position in the foretop. Immediately afterwards the *Bismarck*'s fire slackened off. For two or three minutes. The German ship's guns could no longer operate in unison. Their salvoes dropped into the sea far away from the target.

In fact the British forces had no other opposition than the wind, which piled up the clouds of smoke so that it was impossible for the time being to observe the target. But the radar scanners took care of that...

Further British reinforcements arrived. From the east came the cruiser *Dorsetshire* and opened fire from a range of 20,000 yards.

The British sailors were kept informed of the progress of the battle over the loudspeakers. They answered every announcement with hurrahs. There was no hope for the enemy!

The *Hood* was avenged.

The *Bismarck*'s fire grew more and more erratic. The end must come at any moment. Any moment now the British units would be able to draw even closer to the enemy flagship and fire their torpedoes at the wreck. It didn't matter how long the battle lasted. Battle? It was target practice! Until the *Bismarck* vanished for ever beneath the mountainous waves, until she burst in pieces.

In an hour, or perhaps two, the victory would be announced by innumerable radios all over the world...

Optimism spread like wildfire. Enthusiasm knew no bounds. The British sailors punched one another in the ribs for joy, turned somersaults, joked, told each other all the things they were going to do during their leave. They behaved exactly as the young men on the other side had behaved three days ago when the *Hood* went to the bottom.

What did they care about the enemy's fate? Whoever does care about the enemy's fate? Victory or death was the watchword on all fronts, on every side. This time the British Navy was victorious. This victory was now unalterable. This time the dying was being done by the other side. This dying was now unalterable. War was laying down its laws. Faithful till death is the slogan of every war, on every side. But in the end death remains faithful to war.

When people go to war, they do not know whether they will win or lose. The only certainty is that many of them will die. On both sides, in various uniforms.

This time it was the Germans' turn, the Germans on the *Bismarck*. Why should the British sailors making merry at their action stations, flushed with victory, think of that? Perhaps in the course of the next few years the war would give many of them opportunity for reflecting upon it. But as a rule such reflections come only at the last moment...

While the sea flamed, while the sky grew dark, while shells burst and men died, only a few miles from the inferno two men drifted on a rubber raft through the raging sea. The cold water had made their bodies stiff. They clutched the leather loops on the raft with their hands. They crouched close together, exhausted and despairing. Like this they were carried along by the sea towards an unknown destination. Perhaps death...

At first they tried to talk. They gave it up. The waves swept over them too often. They swallowed salt water, spat it out, only to swallow more the next moment.

How long had they been drifting? Their eyes were burning, they were caked with salt. Their convulsive grip on the loops took all the feeling from their arms. They felt they were at the end of their strength. But they clung on with a superhuman effort in a state of semi-consciousness. They were flung into the air and hurled down again, drenched and battered by the waves. They were tricked by mirages, tortured by cold, kept alive by hope, brought close to death by fear.

These two nameless men had done something unique, something monstrous. Something that had never happened before in the history of naval warfare, something so unbelievable that a German court martial, generally so resolute, hesitated for months before beginning their trial.

The two men had fled from the *Bismarck*...

They had abandoned their ship, their shipmates, their officers, their posts, their duties in the most fantastic fashion. Perhaps it was only their nerves that drove them to do it. Or desperation. Or an overpowering will to live. Or the opportunity. Or fear...

It happened shortly before the engagement began. The sky was still unbroken grey, everyone gave free rein to his thoughts, everyone was thinking the same thing. The two men were standing on the upper deck, staring out to sea. They had discussed what they were about to do a dozen times. Now, in the last second before the jump, they hesitated.

What immense courage it takes to be so cowardly.

Either quickly or not at all. They must act this minute. Come on, throw the stolen raft overboard. The instant it touched water it would inflate automatically and be ready to carry them. Thirteen feet to the water line. Not bad at all. They must jump far out. As far as possible.

Perhaps the man who jumped one second before the other was thinking of his mother or his wife; or wasn't he thinking at all, did he carry out the decision mechanically, did he flee into life because for hours he had been unable to think of anything but death?

They jumped overboard, grabbed the loops and clung to them. The current quickly carried them away from the *Bismarck*. Had they been spotted by the lookout as they made off? Was their escape being reported to the Captain that very minute? What would he do? Would they be shot down in the water? Would their desertion be reported home by radio? Would the curses of those left behind to die pursue them all their lives?

Nothing happened. No one noticed their amazing flight. It had succeeded – for the moment anyhow. The towering waves swept the deserters farther and farther from the scene of impending disaster. They lost all sense of time. While the infernal rhythm of shot and impact thundered in the background, the sea appeared to grow larger, crueller, more boundless. And the fear from which the had fled grew immeasurably.

It had been like this for hours. Whenever one of them began to lose consciousness the other shouted at him. Wake up! Whatever happens, keep awake!

They tried to sing, but the salt water immediately stopped their mouths. Their eyes were red-rimmed. The life-jackets pressed against their throats. They stared at the horizon and saw ships that were only fog-banks. They saw land. They heard voices. But the same instant they knew their senses were deceiving them.

God above, would this never end? Wasn't this worse than being torn to pieces by a shell?... To drown as cowards – slowly, infinitely slowly? If only they had stayed on the ship! They wanted to yell at one another. They hated each other. They cursed each other.

Then pity soothed them. Self-pity. Then they heard the voices of their families. Their grip on the loops loosened. They immediately clutched them tighter again and clung tight, as tight as they could. But they could feel the strength of their hands diminishing. If their hands had been free, and if they had had the strength, they would have gone for one another, each one shouting the other's miserable cowardice in his face.

Would it have helped the others in any way if two, more men had gone down with the ship? Would it have changed the *Bismarck*'s fate at all if 2,402 men had died instead of only 2,400? Didn't it call for more courage to take your destiny in your own hands and drown in this accursed, unending sea, than to stay on board and wait for a shell?

They told themselves so. They believed it. Perhaps they were right. But what are right and wrong in the face of death? Who can pass judgment? Others, who have never been in this situation, who have never had to practise what they preach? The deserters stifled their consciences. They told themselves they were right.

But the very same moment their eyes came to rest on the raft's empty loops. Then they knew that now or later shipmates would drown because these loops were not there to hold on to...

A little later a German U-boat surfaced just in front of them. The two deserters were too numb even to notice it. They were pulled on board. They were given brandy and cigarettes. People talked to them, heard from them about the *Bismarck*'s death struggle and noted the time.

Several U-boats had been ordered by the German Western Naval Command to hurry to the scene of the engagement and aid the *Bismarck*. But they were on their way back from a sortie and had used up all their torpedoes. They had to stand helplessly by as their comrades fought for their lives.

One of these U-boats picked up the two deserters. The Commander was at once suspicious, but he said nothing. On landing, the two men were arrested and questioned. They contradicted themselves. The time gave them away. It was clear mat they had left the *Bismarck* before being ordered to abandon ship.

It was up to the court martial. It tried the two survivors from the *Bismarck*. No one ever learnt the outcome of this trial. It remained a military secret. To break the oath of secrecy, even accidentally, would be punished by death – as no doubt was the flight of the two men who tried to take their fate in their own hands...

Despite a few scenes of panic the crew of the *Bismarck* stood up to their death struggle with admirable discipline. The wounded men were moved into cover under heavy fire, the survivors of decimated teams found their way to the improvised assembly points with or without orders, everyone threw himself into the fray, handled ammunition, cooled the over-heated gun barrels with a fire-extinguisher, went to the aid of shipmates who were shut in, took the places of the dead at action stations that were bound to be blown up by the enemy's next salvo, or the one after that.

Where officers fell, raw young ABS, whose only claim to leadership was their courage and resolution, took over the command until another officer arrived to replace them. Condemned to die, crowded together, surrounded by the dead, in the hail of enemy shells, the men of the *Bismarck* displayed a moving comradeship that rose far above the patriotic bombast of the daily press and party orators.

From the forward sick-bay Lieutenant-Commander Werner Nobis led a party of volunteer stretcher-bearers into action. The enemy's fire had somewhat abated.

'Come on!' he shouted and forced himself through the hatch. Six men followed him. The enemy units had come so close that their silhouettes stood out clearly above the horizon. Nobis didn't get far. Near the AA batteries lay a Sub-Lieutenant with a pale, twisted child's face.

'Peters!'

'They've got me, sir... Both legs blown off.'

'I'll carry you below.'

'It's not worth it, sir... I shan't last that long.'

My God, what can I do, thought Nobis, how can I help?

Six feet from Peters lay another wounded man, who screamed at regular intervals and might perhaps still be saved.

'Got a cigarette?' asked Peters.

Nobis lit one and pushed it between the Sub-Lieutenant's lips.

'I knew they'd get me... Look at that.'

'I'll get you out of here.'

It will all be over in a minute,' murmured Peters. His voice was so weak that Nobis had to bend right down to catch what he was saying. 'You'll come through, sir... I'm sure of that. If anyone... gets out of this... it will be you... it's all so horrible.'

He groaned and whimpered. His feverish eyes became fixed.

'Say goodbye... to my mother,' he muttered. His wide-open eyes were already glassy. The cigarette stuck between his stiffening lips.

'He's dead, sir,' called a man from the damage control party.

For a few seconds Lieutenant-Commander Nobis thought he was going to suffocate. His throat felt tight, strangled, his mouth dry... This twenty-year-old shot to pieces and his last farewell to his mother... His head was spinning. Nausea crept up from his stomach, the bloody merry-go-round went on turning. Parts of bodies, screams, moans, bursting shells, orders!

In the middle of it all a reproachful voice – Deina's voice: 'I knew what it would be like, I told you so. It's madness what you are doing.'

And again his dying shipmates, screams, shells, the voice of destruction...

The Lieutenant-Commander straightened up and turned to the seaman beside him.

'Bloody hell!' he roared.

The *Bismarck* blazed and shot. The upper works were shattered, two gun turrets silenced, the improvised sick-bays filled to overflowing, the medical supplies used up. There were seven hundred or more dead on board – who was to count them? Hundreds of wounded were screaming, groaning or despairing in silence.

Oels, the Executive Officer, had his head ripped off by a direct hit. Admiral Lütjens was dead. But the Captain still stood on the bridge in the conning-tower.

The enemy's fire grew heavier. Hit after hit Armour plating was red-hot from the innumerable fires, at any moment the heat must reach the magazines and set the ammunition alight – after that, death...

Up above, the colossus was ablaze, up above shells were bursting and men dying – but down below everything was intact. Down below the lights were still burning, the telephone working, the turbines running, cigarettes glowing, rumours spreading, conversation buzzing. The impact of the shells could be heard as though from a great distance. They were indistinguishable from the *Bismarck*'s own guns firing. Gun firing or shell landing, those who heard them could take their choice.

The temperature was normal. The ventilation shafts working. The calm, the order, the composure were ghostly. The officers naturally understood the *Bismarck*'s situation, but they choked back their feelings and took care to disseminate optimism. Brief, laconic reports on the progress of the engagement came over the telephone. But the messages the officers and petty officers passed on were very different from those they received.

On the lower decks men did not know – or did not want to know – what was happening only a few yards away from them. There were 2,400 men on the ship. And it was the turn of those on the upper decks first. But War had not forgotten the others. It was saving them up for the end.

The men in the engine-rooms grew accustomed to the unnatural silence. Every now and then one of them would get rattled and start to shout. But the others quickly shut him up. They talked to one another encouragingly. A few said goodbye to each other, exchanged letters, showed each other photographs of their families once again, and noted down telephone numbers or fooled about. The easiest way to face death is to ignore it. The sailors knew they had no need to run after it. It would come to them of its own accord.

But when, for heaven's sake...?

It was fortunate that the telephone system was still intact. It linked the lower decks in an unnatural and eerie way with the battle. As long as you know what's coming it can't be so bad, they thought, they said, they persuaded themselves.

'Say what you like,' said Able Seaman Lauchs, "it's pretty comfortable down here.'

'Like in an air-raid shelter,' replied Moessmer.

'And it'll stand firm too, the Tommies can go on firing their ruddy shells till they're blue in the face.'

'How long has it been going on now?' asked Pollack.

'Don't know,' answered Lauchs. 'Ask Link, he's got hold of a watch.'

'Well, how long is it till your wedding?'

'About half an hour.' The Leading Seaman was quiet and pale, as though he was suffering from a hangover. But they all had a hangover today. They were all quiet and pale. They were all trying to master their thoughts, but instead were mastered by them.

'You've got a fine wedding-eve behind you,' went on Moessmer.

'For God's sake shut up!' Link was irritated, although he had had a week in which to get used to jokes of this kind.

'You can celebrate your wedding night in the water, chum.'

'You're all invited to it. But don't forget to bring your bathing costumes.'

'What about the mermaids? Do you think they're any good? What do you say, lads?'

'You'll have lost interest by then,' snapped Pollack.

The Second Engineer, Lieutenant Herzog, came into the engine-room on his rounds.

'How are things up above?' the question assailed him from all sides.

'Fine, fine... Any trouble down here?'

'No,' replied Lauchs. 'No trouble. We're just bored.'

'In another hour you'll be able to start playing skat again.'

'If the cards haven't gone sky-high by then.'

'Put them in your pocket, then you can go on playing in heaven.'

Pollack protested vigorously.

'You shouldn't crack jokes about that sort of thing, Lieutenant.'

'All right, don't get so worked up, man... We're not in the Salvation Army.'

'It's a pity we're not,' broke in Moessmer.

'What are things really like up top?' Lauchs asked him once more.

The young officer, who looked just as filthy as his crew, shrugged his shoulders.

'You can imagine it,' he then said dejectedly. 'Bloody awful would be putting it mildly.'

'What about the Tommies?'

'They're just having breakfast. Devil take them.'

'He won't do us the favour,' replied Lauchs.

Conversation flagged. Suddenly there was silence. Only the rolling and pitching could be felt. The men looked at each other. Everyone noticed the other's wavering eyes, everyone thought the same. Pollack shouted it out.

'Now they'll blow up the ship. They'll leave us to drown here like rats. It's all over. They don't give a damn about us. We can go to blazes.'

'Quiet man!' the Lieutenant snapped at him. 'Can't you see what rubbish you're talking? Everything's intact. Even the telephone is still working.'

'Why have they stopped firing?' asked Link.

'There's no question of blowing up the ship,' rejoined Lieutenant Herzog. 'And if they did blow it up, it would take at least half an hour. Then they would blow it up from down below, not up there. You'll have plenty of time to abandon ship in comfort. See?'

'I hope you're right,' answered Lauchs.

The telephone! A petty officer was holding the receiver. The Lieutenant took it and announced himself. Everybody stared at him. The conversation was brief. The Lieutenant hung up.

'Well,' he said, 'who's anxious to go up topside?'

'All of us.'

'Who has had first-aid training?'

'All of us,' said Lauchs once more.

The Lieutenant thought for a moment, then turned to the Petty Officer: 'How many men can you spare at the outside?'

'Three.'

The officer looked from one to the other.

'It won't be much fun... Lauchs and Moessmer, get ready to go. Who else shall we take?'

'Link, in honour of the day?'

Link nodded.

'Well, gentlemen, no time for goodbyes... See you later!'

The three men went without a word...

The *Bismarck* was only firing isolated shots at the *King George V*. The *Rodney* was no longer under fire at all. *Norfolk* and *Dorsetshire* drew near the German flagship. The British units had temporarily to cease fire, because the clouds of cordite smoke belching from the gun muzzles made it impossible to observe the fall of shot.

The Commander of the *Rodney*, Captain Dalrymple-Hamilton, whose son was serving as a mid-shipman aboard the *King George V*, decided on his own initiative to put about and so attack the *Bismarck* from the bows with a full broadside.

Now the *Rodney* was closest to the enemy, and the German flagship turned her spasmodic fire upon her.

A few salvoes fell dangerously close. But the British had no more fear. The Gunnery Officer could see through his glasses. The *Bismarck* would soon fall silent altogether. Then the torpedoes would be made ready for the death blow.

The battle had lasted two hours already. It was incredible what the German flagship could stand. The British were firing from every barrel. The colossus must sink! What the hell could it be made of. Was German steel different from ours? Was their steel stronger than our shells? Why did they go on fighting at all? They hadn't a chance! All hell must be loose on the other side. Reports kept coming in all the time: fire observed aft, at the foretop, by the jack, amidships. Direct hit on the upper works.

The gunnery was dead accurate. No complaint at all. The shells were boring into the armour plating incessantly.

Admiral Tovey was resolved to bring matters to a conclusion as quickly as possible – because of his fuel shortage. The reports he was receiving showed that there was nothing further to be done with shells.

The torpedoes were armed.

Else Birken, the bride of Leading Seaman Link, had a ten-minutes' walk to the town hall. Should she have waited with the wedding till he came home on leave? Heavens, how differently she had pictured the day!

Now the moment had come at last she felt sad. She should have had a white dress like other girls. Bridesmaids should have carried her train, and after the church wedding the young bridegroom should have thrown coins to the youngsters; then they should have gone to the photographer and smiled earnestly on the photograph that would hang for the rest of their lives over the sofa in the parlour...

That was how it should have been...

Nonsense, Else told herself, that's all right in peace-time. Now there's a war on. Other girls didn't manage to get married at all. When the war was over they would be all right. Hans would take over his father's grocery business. He wouldn't earn a great deal. But it would be enough for two, three or four.

We are simpletons, Else mused on. We could have waited. There's no hurry. People are already making jokes, but they don't know how silly and unfounded their jokes are. Suppose he doesn't come back?

The newspapers were full of articles about the *Bismarck*. He will come back, she told herself. He must come back! And this cursed war, that has put itself in the way of our happiness, must also be over one day.

Ridiculous, this empty chair beside her. The Mayor stood up and began his speech.

'Honoured bridal pair,' he began, and those present stifled a grin. Then the staunch fellow talked about fatherland, duty and the nation. Else wasn't really listening. This stuff had been poured out over the radio and in the newspapers for eight years; her thoughts were miles away.

The Mayor knew his speech by heart. That took some of the edge off it. Over his head hung a picture of Hitler. The sun was shining on the left side. The light made it seem larger, as though the man whose likeness hung in every tavern, every school, every office had a swollen cheek.

It would go well with his voice, thought Else for a second.

Then she had her thoughts under control again and forced herself to listen.

For the first time in her life she signed herself Link. Then she embraced her parents-in-law.

Else Birken did not know that at that moment she was already a widow, before ever becoming a wife. She had married a dead man, long before it became the fashion, as the war went on, to marry dead men....

At first everything was quite easy for Lauchs, Link and Moessmer. The gangways were lit and clear of obstacles, there was no disorder, no panic. Then they met the first wounded, climbed through the twisted hatches, accustomed themselves to the smoke and stench, stumbled over pipes and dangling wires, fought with darkness and fear, learnt to step over the dead, saw chaos and were bewildered by it.

On one of the upper decks they found a seaman cowering helplessly against a bulkhead.

'What's the matter, man?' asked Lauchs.

'Both heels blown off.'

'That's not so bad. We'll carry you to the dressing-station.'

'Dressing-station?' groaned the seaman. 'There isn't any dressing-station. There's nothing left. It's shut.'

'Rubbish. If you stay here you'll peg out.'

'I want to peg out.'

They dragged the man along for a few yards, but he struggled desperately.

'Leave him,' said Lauchs eventually.

Soon afterwards they realized how right the wounded man had been...

They came upon an emergency dressing-station. Lauchs went up to a Surgeon Commander.

'Where shall we report?' he asked.

'Report where you like,' answered the surgeon roughly. He was working in his shirtsleeves. His hair was hanging down over his face. He was gasping with the effort and cursing. But when he spoke to the wounded his voice suddenly changed, becoming soft, almost gentle. The three men stood around awkwardly, tried to look away, but couldn't control their eyes.

'I can't stand any more of this,' said Link. 'I can't move another inch. I can't look any more. Stop! Stop this madness!'

'Pull yourself together,' Moessmer snapped at him.

'I can't carry on,' groaned Link.

The British guns opened up again. Someone was waving a torch about.

'The emergency lights will be on in a moment,' shouted a Chief Petty Officer.

'How much morphia have we left?' asked a surgeon. 'Leave him where he is, he's dead. Come on, don't stand there like a dummy,' he shouted at Moessmer the next moment. 'Take him outside!'

'Where to?'

'Wherever there's room!'

Link was at the end of his tether. Moessmer yelled at him, but he took no notice. Then the emergency light went on. The Leading Seaman was murmuring to himself. He didn't realize that he was praying. He was praying aloud. Over and over again, until the words took on meaning, for him and for the others standing near. He was startled by his own voice, stopped, as though he felt ashamed, and then spoke loud and clear.

'Our father which art in heaven, hallowed be thy name...'

A wounded man screamed. At the top of his voice. A despairing shriek.

'No,' he yelled, 'I won't let you cut off my leg!'

'Thy kingdom come, thy will be done, on earth as it is in heaven...'

A shell landed; Exploded. There were screams. Pandemonium. Curses.

'Shut up!' bawled Moessmer. 'Shut up!'

'Leave him alone!' Lauchs flared at him.

'Give us today our daily bread, and forgive us our trespasses as we forgive them that trespass against us.'

'He'll drive us all scatty,' roared Moessmer again.

But all at once he was alone. Scorn, fear, shame had vanished. Wounded men were moaning, hoarse commands penetrated from outside. But for an instant, a very brief, very strange instant, thoughts were lifted above all that. Suddenly the narrow emergency dressing-station became a place of worship.

The prayer rose above the fumes of the room. Above fear. Above death. Above this inferno...

'Lead us not into temptation, but deliver us from evil. Amen.'

Link's voice had grown firmer. Moessmer was suddenly carried away with indignation.

'Don't forget the Church gives its blessing to armaments on both sides!'

Lauchs put his arms round his shoulders. The good-time boy, whose ideas of life ranged between alcohol and cheap women, eating and joking, reached out beyond himself and carried the others with him by his self-control, by his voice.

'Listen,' he said. 'If there is a God, one day those who are guilty of all this will find their hands rotting off in punishment. Be sure of that.' He turned to Link. 'Are you coming with me?'

'Yes,' said Link.

It all happened in a flash. Lauchs was in front, behind him came Link and Moessmer. They had conquered their horror.

'Here,' said Lauchs. 'We'd better start here.'

They were standing close together. A shell whined towards them. All three flung themselves to the ground. The shell landed right in the middle of them. A direct hit.

The three who had come up from the engine-room to help their shipmates were now beyond help themselves...

Leading Seaman Penzlau was one of those men who no longer sought cover, who sat around dully waiting for the end. He crouched down beside a dead body, leaned back, closed his eyes, listened to the shells landing. But while death mowed down his shipmates who sought cover all around him, he was protected from the splinters, at least for the time being.

When he came up on deck his mind just went blank. He saw everything as though through a veil of blood. He stumbled on, hearing commands without reacting to them. He learnt, with disgust, to climb over the dead. He looked for a space, found it and there waited for the end. Penzlau had never thought about the war. He had come straight on to the *Bismarck* after completing his basic training, and like his shipmates he allowed himself to be stuffed with confident belief in victory. He had nothing against the English, couldn't have anything against them because he didn't know them. The horror stories served up to him in the papers left him cold; as a rule he didn't even read them.

But now, surrounded by chaos, among the ruins of vanished glory, during these endless minutes that preceded his last breath, he hated the British passionately.

Not because they were blowing the *Bismarck* to, pieces, not because they were attacking with overwhelmingly superior forces, not because they were sending in their death-bringing salvoes from a safe distance, no... because they were taking so long over it, because it was all going so slowly, because they were destroying the *Bismarck* piecemeal, instead of getting it over quickly.

Who could expect Leading Seaman Penzlau to think fairly at a time like this? He simply concentrated all his hatred of the atrocious war on the nearest enemy – the Tommies. So he sat there waiting, unfeeling, burnt out, turned to stone, dull-witted – waiting for death.

But death didn't come, wouldn't come; it was grabbing others, who were trying to escape it. It was saving the Leading Seaman for later. It had special plans for him. A particular agony, a final torment.

'Come with me, mate,' Bauer II shouted to him.

'No.'

'Don't you want to go home?'

'Home?' replied Penzlau contemptuously. 'Home?'

That was the cue for his suffering to begin. Now it hurt terribly. He opened his eyes but saw nothing. His thoughts went racing back to his last leave. Eight days special leave, because he had passed out top of his class. He was amazed to find himself sitting in the train. The engine went far too slowly for him, but at last, after travelling for hours, he arrived at his little Silesian home town.

He had twenty minutes to walk. He did it in ten. He raced along with curious jumping steps. A Chief Petty Officer shouted at him for not saluting. But he took no notice and hurried on, and the Chief Petty Officer didn't feel like running after him.

Penzlau was hurrying to Ema, his pretty young wife, to whom he had been married, according to the marriage certificate, for a year and a half, but in reality for barely three weeks. God, how surprised she would be! She was bound to be in bed, asleep, and it would be some time before she woke up and sleepily opened the door to him. They had a pleasant little two-room flat on the outskirts of the town, of which the Leading Seaman dreamed whenever his duties left him time to do so.

He stood panting at the front door. He paused for a moment, to get his breath back before meeting Erna. Happiness flowed through him hot and tempestuous, as he pressed the electric bell. His flat was on the second floor. He heard the muffled ringing of the bell. He took his finger off. He didn't want Ema to get a fright. He didn't want her to be startled out of her sleep.

Nothing happened. He rang again.

Again nothing. Nothing at all.

Something must be wrong. The whole house would be woken by the noise. And so it was. Frau Meierling on the first floor poked her tousled head out of the window. She looked ghostly in the moonlight, with gleaming curlers in her hair.

'What's the matter?' she asked angrily. Then she recognized Penzlau. 'Oh, it's you... Wait a minute and I'll open the door.'

He went up the stairs in a few bounds.

'Where's my wife?' he panted.

'Come in,' answered Frau Meierling. 'Sit down. Here, I've got a cigarette for you, and I'll give you a drink too.'

'What's up?'

She looked at him seriously and pityingly, without replying. Then she turned away and toyed with the bottle, poured out and spilt a few drops on the highly polished table. She didn't even notice. If she doesn't notice that, she must be pretty upset about something, thought Penzlau mechanically.

'I can't tell you,' replied Frau Meierling. 'I simply can't tell you.'

'What is it then?' asked Penzlau. A horrible feeling was slowly creeping up his spine. His mouth went dry and stale. Without thinking, he reached for the bottle, but it didn't help, the stale taste remained.

'Where's my wife?' he asked again.

'I can't tell you,' answered Frau Meierling, and straight away began to tell him. That Ema was working in an all-night bar, for some weeks already, that men, generally soldiers, brought her to the door, that recently a civilian, a tall, imposing man, had been round, that he, too, had brought Ema to the door, that they had stood for a long time in the porch, and that she, Frau Meierling, had heard every word they said, and that then the two of them...

'No, I can't tell you, Herr Penzlau,' the woman said once more.

The Leading Seaman was no longer listening. He jumped up, without saying goodbye, and went back along the long dark street, not as fast as a few minutes ago nor in such a hurry to reach his goal, though he had a goal – the Cockatoo Bar. The porter looked at him suspiciously. Other ranks were rare in this expensive establishment. Penzlau handed over his coat and walked down a narrow passage. Thick runners deadened his footsteps. Mirrors hung on the walls. They reflected the pale face of a German sailor. He walked across the room. Heavily made-up girls were sitting at the tables chatting with officers, who eyed him just as suspiciously as the liveried porter.

Penzlau found his way to the little bar with the certainty of a sleep-walker. Two girls were sitting behind it, the one on the right was Ema. She was perched on a stool, one leg crossed over the other, smoking a cigarette in a long holder. She was wearing a dress Penzlau had never seen before, a thin, low-cut dress of cheap red silk. She was talking to a man who leaned far over towards her. She hit him on the fingers, but the man smiled. It was a satisfied smile.

Penzlau sat down on a stool. Erna pushed the menu over to him.

'What shall I get you?' she enquired mechanically.

Then she recognized him. Her mask-like smile convulsed, her cigarette-holder trembled. She was frightened. Penzlau could see that even by this artistically dim light, which was specially designed to lend life to pallid faces.

'It's you,' she said. Her voice sounded hoarse. She toyed nervously with a silver cocktail-shaker, although nobody had ordered a cocktail.

The man sitting opposite Ema was suddenly in a, great hurry. He stood up, said goodbye briefly and left, without even paying. He avoided the Leading Seaman's eyes, as though he had a bad conscience. At first he walked slowly, but as soon as he was a few yards away he positively sprinted to the exit.

'Why didn't you write to me you had leave?' asked Erna.

'Why didn't you tell me you worked in an all-night bar?'

'I had to do something... It was so dull. I couldn't stick it any longer, always between those four walls.'

'In the past you liked it there.'

'In the past,' she reiterated, 'in the past everything was different.'

'Oh,' he said. It sounded hollow and despairing.

He had to wait three hours. He had to watch the officers go up to the bar, eye him contemptuously and pass vapid remarks to his wife. He saw how she smiled, crossed one leg over the other, leaned forward and drank with them. He heard the stupid bar-room catch phrases and tasteless platitudes. And he thought, that isn't Ema, my wife. She has become a different person. That is a woman I want nothing more to do with.

They walked along side by side through the cold morning mist without speaking. Ema unlocked the door. Frau Meierling's shadow disappeared from the window. They mounted the stairs and were in their own kingdom. But this kingdom had meanwhile been conquered by another.

The week dragged slowly by. Once or twice Leading Seaman Penzlau toyed with the idea of going back at once. But he didn't want his shipmates to see that something was wrong. He wanted to lock his shame up inside himself.

She went with him to the station and stood by the train, tapping her feet, as though in a hurry to see him go. They talked trivialities. Neither of them said what they both knew: that they had nothing more to say to one another. That it was all over.

The train pulled out of the station. Penzlau stared out of the windows as long as he could see Ema. He saw how she turned on her heel and hurried back to the barrier.

Then he returned to the *Bismarck*, and she put out on her first sortie. Penzlau was almost relieved when he heard they were going.

'Come on!' Bauer II shouted to him once more. 'Don't sit there like a stuffed dummy! You can't just wait around till you kick the bucket!'

The Leading Seaman shook off his memories with a jerk. He looked at his dead shipmates lying everywhere; they suddenly seemed to be spinning wildly round him with contorted, grinning faces. He looked , through the veil of blood, pressed his lips together and looked almost curiously at the bursting shells. He watched others dying to right and left of him.

'My wife,' he said, '...that was my wife,' he muttered to himself.

Leading Seaman Penzlau's suffering lasted exactly sixty-four minutes.

Then came a direct hit.

There was little or nothing left of him...

The blood trickled down sticky and slow, through hatches and gangways on to the tween-decks, where it gathered in horribly colourful puddles: the blood of the dead, the dying, the maimed, the amputated – the blood of officers, petty officers and ratings, who were lying jumbled together in dozens, in hundreds between the gaping muzzles of the guns, with waxen faces and wide-open, staring eyes. Every now and then the sea sent a breaker over the side, the salt water washed away the ghastly pools, the wave carried off a pile of dead.

The men who came up on deck from their electrically-lit and heated underworld screamed in horror, vomited and fled back... to where there was no possible way of escape. But where was there any way of escape?

The British guns continued to thunder, the shells to shriek across towards the *Bismarck*. Her seamen continued to receive the splinters in their bodies, silently collapse and die. Able Seaman Grabler had joined up with a group of survivors from decimated teams in the mess. Chairs and tables had been knocked over. The till lay on the floor with blood-smeared notes scattered all round.

A petty officer bent down, picked them up and thrust them into his pocket. He grinned crazily, then counted the money. What for? What use could he make of it now, when there was barely time for a last prayer? The men, of whom there were now six or seven, made for the upper deck. As they climbed through the hatch those in front tried to turn back, but those behind were pushing forward. The British had paused for a breather.

'Now's our chance!' shouted Grabler. 'Go on, don't be yellow. We must get up on deck!'

The petty officer in front turned round, his face twisted into a grimace. 'Then you can go first,' he stammered hoarsely.

Grabler clambered up the iron rungs, crawled through the narrow hatch, shut his eyes, opened them again and stared at the mountains of dead lying in front of him, packed together like ration bread. Dead shipmates, ripped to pieces by shells. Grabler hurried on. He tripped over limbs. An atrocious scene. A head on its own. With wide, staring eyes. Grabler saw it, turned away, looked back at it. Then he went berserk, rushed at the man nearest to him, a Lieutenant, seized him with his right hand, shook him to and fro and yelled at the top of his voice:

'You filthy murderers! You swine! That's all you can do! You're not capable of anything else! Just look around. There's your war! Murderers, filthy murderers! ...Faithful till death!' His screeching voice cracked.

'Pull yourself together, man!' the officer shouted to him.

A shell. Both men threw themselves to the ground. The officer for the last time. He was lucky, he died instantly. Grabler lay unconscious. The men who had come up from the mess with him raised him cautiously. Pain brought the Leading Seaman to his senses again. He opened his eyes.

'Be careful,' he groaned. 'The pain is terrible.'

Then he stared at the bleeding stump of his arm and saw the right sleeve of his uniform lying on the deck with the clenched hand projecting, the hand with which he had been shaking the officer this way and that a few seconds before, the hand he had stretched out a thousand times in the so-called German greeting. He would never again be able to raise it in the Hitler salute. And in an hour he would be a dead man, one of many, one under a mountain of others.

Dead, bled to death, washed away... this was the fate of the crew of the biggest and most modern battleship in the world.

The *Bismarck* was listing heavily to port. The main mast had snapped. The upper works were ablaze. Anti-aircraft ammunition that had been lying around was exploding. 'D' turret had a burst barrel. Its side was battered by heavy shells. They rebounded from the turret itself. The sea was washing over the upper-deck. Behind a 6-inch turret lay a pile of bodies as high as the turret. The men had sought cover behind it and had been torn to pieces by the rebounding splinters.

All of a sudden the sun came out and shone as on any other day, casting its beam on the dead, the wounded and the despairing. The enemy fire stopped.

The *Bismarck* had fired her last shell. She could no longer defend herself. Why did the Captain still hesitate? Why didn't he blow up the wreck? Why didn't he give the word for the survivors to jump overboard?

Communications between most of the control points had been broken. A few officers sent messengers to the lower decks to warn the men that the ship was about to be scuttled. Some decks were completely cut off. The sailors in these sections were condemned to go down with the ship. Perhaps that was why they delayed over the act of self-destruction. Damage control parties were trying to open the hatches with acetylene torches. The men were now standing in dozens on the upper deck, making use of the break in the fighting to consider how they should go overboard when the order came to abandon ship. Pilots were appointed to guide the men to the two or three hatches to the upper deck that were still intact. All officers who could be spared were sent below to prevent panic.

But nothing was known yet about the blowing up of the ship. Perhaps it was only a rumour. Only one man could give the order – the Captain.

Captain Lindemann delayed as long as he could. For the moment he merely had preparations made.

Messengers were sent to the battle stations that had ceased to answer. The men on deck inflated their life-jackets. Many did so too early and got wedged in the narrow hatches.

Leading Seaman Rzonca stood in front of the last hatchway. In front of him men were working on the hatch-cover with crowbars. Eventually they managed to force it sufficiently wide open to struggle through.

The wounded first. Without being ordered to, the last of the group stayed behind to show the way to those who came later.

'Don't forget to climb out yourself!' Rzonca called to him.

'There's plenty of time. You'll be there much too early,' rejoined the man.

The slightly wounded were carried over to the lowered rails.

'Wrong side!' roared Lieutenant-Commander Nobis. 'Not on the port side!'

Of course, the waves were coming from this direction and would smash everyone against the hull. But the officer had to tell practically every man individually.

There was silence, an almost ghostly silence. Both sides had ceased firing. Perhaps only for a matter of minutes. The enemy ships were coming closer. Everybody could see them.

Suddenly a single gun began firing. A 4-inch AA gun that had not yet run out of ammunition. The fellows must have gone crazy! They shot wildly merely to calm their nerves or to make sure that the *Bismarck* had literally fought to the last shell!

'Cease fire!' bawled Lieutenant-Commander Nobis.

The British had already replied. Everyone leaped for cover.

Nobis was standing amidships. Crash. Everyone looked around when the smoke had cleared.

'Anyone hurt?' someone called out.

'No.'

'Where's the Lieutenant-Commander?'

Only then did they notice that Nobis had disappeared.

The blast from the exploding shell had blown Lieutenant-Commander Werner Nobis overboard. Like a scrap of paper. He struck the water hard, but felt the blow only subconsciously. His life-jacket kept him afloat. For a few seconds he fainted, then the ice-cold sea brought him round. It hurled him into troughs, bore him up over crests, got into his eyes and into the pores of his skin and carried him farther and farther from the *Bismarck*.

Nobis swallowed water. It tasted of oil and salt. He spat it out, vomited and stared at a dead body floating along beside him with a disfigured face and the already rigid hand stretched out to the sky as though to salute the Lieutenant-Commander for the last time. Gradually Nobis overcame his horror. All the time on the verge of fainting again, he adapted his swimming movements to the waves. His head was aching, his eyes were smarting, his limbs growing numb, his thoughts in a whirl. He was shaking by coughing. His strength was ebbing. Up and down, like the switch-back at a fair – the fair of war, death, nerves and senses. The frail will to live was fighting against the elements, against the ocean.

Measureless time. How long could a man hold out? Not long, thank God! I mustn't give up, I mustn't, he thought. He drifted towards a huge patch of oil. He must avoid it at all costs. He thrashed about with his arms and legs, gasping for breath. Oil gums up the eyes, blocks the pores of the skin. That means suffocation...

He drifted closer and closer to the oil. It was useless trying to swim with this sea running – then a wave lifted him up and hurled him away, a few seconds later he had been carried yards past the deadly patch of oil. A name sprang to his mind – Bauer; yes, of course, Able Seaman Bauer had been shipwrecked and swallowed fuel oil. It turned him into a permanent invalid, for ever surrounded by doctors. He had to be artificially fed – a living corpse.

Anything rather than that! Wherever he looked he saw greasy patches, large and small pools of oil, shimmering in poisonous iridescence. He raised his head as far out of the water as possible. If only the head-rest of the life-jacket didn't press so hard against the back of his neck!

He found himself in a whirlpool. A merry-go-round, he thought, this is the end. He lay on his back. The sea granted him a breather. He saw the *Bismarck* in front of him, six or seven hundred yards away. He could see the men running to and fro on the upper deck, agitated little black dots. He felt how alone he was, how lonely, how helpless.

The British had stopped firing. What was there left for them to shoot at? The *Bismarck* was only a battered hulk. What on earth are they all doing in the bows? thought Nobis. They must be going to blow her up now. Then they will find out what the final hellish torment is like, in the water.

The wind had blown the clouds apart. The sun was poised in the sky, glowing red, as though to cast a brighter and more revealing light upon the inferno. From somewhere on the horizon came the faint sound of a gun firing. Or perhaps it was an illusion. Have I come to that? thought Nobis. Soon I shall see land or a ship or a lifeboat. That will be the last stage before the end. You can't get away with it twice, mused Nobis. You can't be the only survivor from a wreck twice. Last time it was much easier, much more innocuous. The sea had carried him to Portugal and Deina...

Now the sea had him in its clutches again. Death too? Then he saw his father before him, old, grey-haired and sad. Nobis saw the painful smile, the helpless gestures. He heard the quiet, shy voice.

'I would rather you hadn't come back till after the war, my boy.'

A whirlpool dragged him down into the depths. Nobis swallowed water, thrashed about, fought with the sea – there was no more time for gloomy thoughts. His eyes were smarting. The salt stuck them together. He gradually managed to get them open again.

A noise. What was it? A mirage? A ghastly figment of the imagination?

No, there it was again, quite close to him – it must be a destroyer. It was racing towards him full speed. Nobis stared at the British ship. He could see the sailors on deck. They couldn't help spotting him. He shouted. Would they hear him? Would they see him? Would they help him?

The destroyer came closer. Now they must slow down, throw him a line and haul him up. They couldn't leave him to perish! That was impossible!

No human being could do that. And they were human beings, even if they were on the other side.

The destroyer shot past. Like lightning. At full speed.

So that's what it's like, thought Nobis bitterly. He grew drowsy, resigned. So that's what dying is like....

Admiral Sir John Tovey gazed through his glasses and shook his head. It was incredible. The *Bismarck*, that shattered, burning wreck wouldn't go down. Practically every salvo had hit the mark. The return fire had long since fallen silent, the mast was snapped off, the superstructure in ruins, but the flag still flew.

'Get closer!' ordered the Admiral. 'Torpedoes away!' The *Rodney* fired her torpedoes at the German flagship from a range of 3,000 yards. One of them struck the *Bismarck* amidships. The *Norfolk* also fired four torpedoes at the wreck. She observed one hit – but the *Bismarck* didn't sink.

More torpedoes were on their way. The *Dorsetshire* was closing in for a torpedo attack.

Another torpedo struck the *Bismarck* from a range of 4,000 yards. Admiral Tovey could wait no longer. He feared a German air attack. But still more he feared the shortage of fuel. Even before the engagement was over he ordered the *Rodney* to return to base.

But the *Bismarck* was still afloat. Numberless shells and torpedoes had failed to sink her. For Sir John every shot more represented a waste of ammunition, every second more an increase in his fuel difficulties. Should he leave the wreck to drift? Should he report to London that he had defeated the German flagship but not destroyed it? After this unparalleled seven days' chase he had closed with the enemy and reduced him to a wreck, but' he had not sent him to the bottom. He could now observe the effects of his concentrated shelling with the naked eye. He stood irresolute on his undamaged bridge. Perhaps the *Dorsetshire* would bring it off.

'Get closer, get closer,' he radioed his cruiser.

The *Dorsetshire* had two torpedoes left. From a range of 2,500 yards she couldn't miss. But the torpedoes of the other units had also hit the target, yet the *Bismarck* hadn't sunk.

At 10.36 a.m. a torpedo from the *Dorsetshire* hit the *Bismarck* on her port beam.

Admiral Tovey could see the men on the other side running helplessly this way and that on the deck. He could see the guns pointing their barrels in all directions. He could see the fires and the billowing smoke. Through his glasses he observed the hundreds of dead – his work, the work of his floating death factory, made by men for the destruction of men.

But here it was not a question of men, but of war. Of the harvest of war that enriched death's kingdom by millions. Did his enemy, Admiral Lütjens, who had died that very day, think of the last despairing sigh, the last terror, the last horror, when he blew up the *Hood* a few days earlier?

No, such thoughts are outside an Admiral's competence. He conducts a perfect operation of destruction, as learnt at Staff College. He is merely doing his duty – Admirals on both sides assiduously do their duty. This duty costs a few thousand men their lives on each side. But human lives are cheap in time of war...

More and more men had fought their way through on to the *Bismarck*'s upper deck. In the lower decks, in the engine-rooms the lights were still burning, the turbines still rotating, the men standing lost at their posts waiting for the end. Contact with the bridge had been broken. Lieutenant-Commander Junack, the engineer officer of the 10th Half-Division responsible for damage control, who had been working frenziedly with his party for hours, sent a messenger to the Commander. That was just after 10 a.m. The man had not returned. The tall, slim officer went himself. He fought his way up to the deck, saw the carnage, realized the hopelessness of the situation and resolved to act on his own initiative.

He made up his mind to order the scuttling of the ship. He gathered together his most reliable men, suppressed panic, ordered the slightly wounded to be taken up on deck and sent messengers through the whole ship with the warning:

'Ship will be blown up in five minutes. All hands on the upper deck.'

Junack went down below again, looked at the time, sent away all the men who could be spared.

'All clear,' reported Chief Mechanician Fischer, whose job it was to light the fuse.

Cold water would pour into the turbines, the hull would fill up like a sponge and then go down. Before this happened the survivors of the crew must be over-board, in order not to be dragged down by the sink-ing giant's suction.

Plan X this was called during the working-up...

'Wait another eight minutes,' Lieutenant-Commander Junack ordered the Chief Mechanician.

A group of five or six men were inflating their life-jackets.

'Take your time, gentlemen,' said the officer. 'Inflate your life-jacket after you've reached the upper deck. Otherwise you won't get through the hatches. There's no hurry. We shall wait till you're all topside.... Lindenberg, take charge of the group!'

'Aye-aye, sir.'

Time was pressing. On the *Bismarck* they did not know how desperately short of fuel the British were. The ship was to be blown up to prevent boarding. But how many men were still shut in? How many were isolated from the rest and totally unaware that the ship was going to be blown up? And what had happened to the Captain? Was he alive? Would he approve Plan X, or was it still too early?

I must act, Lieutenant-Commander Junack told himself. He nodded to Chief Mechanician Fischer.

'Come up right away!' he said. He did his best to radiate calm. And he succeeded. Once more he was able to prevent a panic flight along the gangways. Wherever he appeared the men grew calmer, as though infected by his *sang-froid*. The crew still maintained discipline.

The Lieutenant-Commander went round the lower decks, gave the order to withdraw and waited for a few minutes. He looked at his watch. At any moment an explosion would tell him that the charge had been detonated. Then he would have a few minutes in which to get off the ship. The *Bismarck* wouldn't go down all that quickly...

Fischer came to the engine-room with two men. It was already empty. The ratings had left their posts according to orders. The charge lay ready. It could be fused with a couple of movements. The designers of the *Bismarck* had thought of everything. Even of this. Even of self-destruction.

'There we are,' said Fischer. 'I'll see to the rest on my own. Go up on deck.'

'What do you mean?' asked an AB

'I'm staying down here,' answered Fischer. 'I shall detonate by hand.'

'You must be crazy!' cried a horrified petty officer.

The Chief Mechanician looked at his watch. Another two minutes. The last 120 seconds of his life, to which he was so much attached. He thought of his mother, his family, his little house, his brothers and sisters. Another 110 seconds.

Fischer turned to his men.

'Get going!' he shouted. His voice broke.

Only now did the men realize what the Chief Mechanician was planning to do. That he meant to die. By his own hand. By his own demolition charge. That he wanted a quick end...

'I shan't go,' sobbed the AB

'Yes, you will,' replied Fischer firmly. His face twitched. Was he more afraid of tears than of death?

The three men stared at the charge, at the ridiculous little cartridge, the tiny lever, the fuse, the dynamite container. They listened to the ghostly silence. Seconds passed. Words stuck in their throats. Their eyes ached. Their temples hammered. Thoughts paralysed their brains.

The AB was weeping unrestrainedly like a child.

'You've got a wife and children,' said Petty Officer Knebel to his superior. 'Think of them.'

Fischer nodded distractedly, as though he hadn't understood the words. His face was pale, his hands trembling. But a desperate courage had taken posses-sion of him. It controlled him and drove him on.

'This is it,' he said in a low voice. He indicated the AB and was about to shake hands with the Petty Officer, but his arm wouldn't move, as though it feared the emotional gesture.

'He's still so young,' said Fischer.

'Come on,' Petty Officer Knebel shouted at the took hold of him, forced him over to the bulk-head and made him climb through. He clambered after him, drove the youngster across the deck, then stood still, panting, and drew a deep breath.

At that second the charge exploded.

One more death on the *Bismarck*.

Surgeon-Commander Thiele, on the shelter-deck, did not look up when he received warning that the ship was going to be scuttled. He was bandaging the stump of an arm, calling out to another wounded man and already looking at his next patient. He was toiling, cursing, sweating, shouting and comforting as far as he could.

'Sir,' said the Sick Berth Petty Officer repeatedly to Thiele, 'the ship is going down in ten minutes.'

'I don't care,' the Surgeon-Commander snapped at him. 'Don't stand around, man! Get a move on, get them all out on the upper deck... You can leave those four in the corner.'

'Don't leave us alone,' cried the man with no arms.

'Easy,' replied the Surgeon-Commander. 'You'll all get out of here.'

'Water,' begged one of the four in the corner, whose belly had been ripped open by a shell splinter.

'In a minute.' Thiele signed to one of the stretcher bearers.

'But I can't stop for that now,' contradicted the man.

'Damn it,' Thiele roared at him, 'do as I tell you!'

Most of the wounded had already been carried up on deck and from there thrown into the water. Many resisted desperately. But it was the only way to save them – if they could be saved at all.

Now they brought along Artificer Petty Officer Hauser. Both legs gone. The Surgeon-Commander bent down to him.

'Listen. There's no time to bandage you up. Do you understand?'

'Yes.'

'The cold water may stop the bleeding. It's a chance. You must simply use every ounce of will-power and keep telling yourself you want to live. Do you understand?'

'Yes, sir.'

'Take him out!'

Now, amidst so much death, in this inferno, on this burning, stinking, self-destroying wreck, there took place an almost inconceivable miracle of life. Artificer Petty Officer Hauser was thrown, as carefully as possible, into the ocean. He had an iron determination to live. For an eternity he fought against fainting. He opposed death with tremendous force of will. He stood up to the pain. He refused to think of the fact that he was a man without legs. The waves carried him over to the other side, straight up to the *Dorsetshire*, the enemy cruiser. British seamen spotted the maimed man. Hauser had the strength to hold on to one of the lines thrown over the side. Dozens of other sailors, for whom the next few seconds meant life or death, gave up their places and used their last ounce of strength to help their legless shipmate. He was pulled aboard, immediately operated on, and... he escaped with his life.

The stretcher-bearer parties functioned perfectly during these last seconds before the *Bismarck* went down. A thousand hands set to, although the wreck was on the point of blowing up.

Dozens of wounded were carried from the sick-bay even after the explosion. Many of them resisted, screamed, groaned, struck out. The worst moment came when they were on the upper deck and ready to be thrown into the sea. Several of the stretcher bearers went back to fetch more wounded, in spite of their own fear of getting off the ship too late. What was the use of throwing people overboard? What help was there for anyone left on the *Bismarck*?

'Leave them where they are,' said Surgeon-Commander Thiele in an undertone. 'Give me the morphia... All there is. No, don't bother about sterilizing the needle. Get going, Weber, it's high time you were off.'

'But what's going to happen to you, sir?' asked the Sick Berth Petty Officer.

'I give you three guesses,' answered Surgeon-Commander Thiele.

He was alone with the groaning, moaning wounded. He had not yet had time to think of himself. Not even of what lay ahead. Nor of his home. For hours he had been acting as though under a hypnotic compulsion. But now these last terrible seconds, the feeling that the ship was heling further and further over, sinking deeper and deeper, that more and more water was pouring in, that the poor helpless, defenceless creatures beside him were growing increasingly afraid of him, exasperated him, made him suddenly hate and fear death. He wanted to be up and gone. There was still time. He could still reach the upper deck.

Surgeon-Commander Thiele had done his duty and more than his duty. No one could expect him to go down with this battered wreck, to die with these wounded men who had been marked down for death beyond hope of saving hours ago. He looked into the grey drawn faces. He saw the twitching lips, heard the screams. He glimpsed the crazily staring eyes – and he stood as though rooted to the spot.

Surgeon-Commander Thiele stayed.

A recollection of his first lecture at medical school flashed through his mind. The old professor, his eyes shining, the glow of health on his cheeks, stood on the platform. 'You have chosen the finest subject of study there is or ever can be. You have enrolled in the service of mankind. I greet you as allies in the battle against sickness, suffering and death. There is no finer vocation, even though it is sometimes hard, even though victory and defeat follow one another in rapid succession. Always remember that"

The Surgeon-Commander had the syringe in his hand. He went over to the first of the wounded men. The latter immediately awoke from his semi-coma.

'Shall I get off the boat too?' he asked.

'Yes,' replied Surgeon-Commander Thiele, 'we shall all get off.'

The man leaned back and smiled. The surgeon carefully introduced the needle and expelled the contents of the syringe, quite slowly. As he did so he watched his patient, thought to himself, that will be enough, withdrew the needle, went on to the next man, did the same, hurried on to the one after that and came to the fourth man, who had been calmly following all his movements.

This man knew what was going on. He smiled gratefully; helplessly he stretched out his hand to shake the doctor's. But Surgeon-Commander Thiele had no time to spare. He only nodded to him.

'It'll soon be over,' he said. 'There's nothing to be afraid of.'

'I'm not afraid,' answered the man slowly.

There was one more to be dealt with. The last injection. Morphia is a blessing. Heavens, a whole city could have been supplied with the ampoules that had been used up during the last few hours.

Now came the worst. Steady! It wasn't so bad. Others had met a much worse fate. He mustn't think. Time was short. Any moment now the water would come pouring in. How many men were still trapped in different parts of the ship? It was no use asking questions now. The time had come to act.

One of the wounded moved. Surgeon-Commander Thiele gave him another injection.

Then it was his turn. He bared his arm, thrust the needle home and squeezed, slowly and carefully, as he had done with his patients. Done it, he said, and thought about something entirely different.

He lay down beside the wounded men, beside the man who had smiled at him so gratefully and who would never wake up again.

Surgeon-Commander Thiele would never wake up again either.

Overboard! But where could they jump? And what was the point of it? Time was short. Most of them stood there as though rooted to the spot. Burger was the first to try. On the port beam, to which the *Bismarck* was listing heavily. He went aft and jumped.

It was all over in two seconds. A wave lifted him up and smashed him with all its force against the hull. Killed outright. Dozens saw it. Hundreds were standing around. Burger was not the only one who met his end that way.

'Jump off from the starboard side,' one man said to the other.

But when they got to the starboard rail their courage failed them.

'I'm not going! Not for anything!' shouted Pollack.'I won't do it!'

'Shut your trap!' a Petty Officer yelled at him. 'You can stay here if you want to, but don't drive everyone else scatty!'

Fresh men came up on deck.

'Has the ship been blown up yet or hasn't it?' they asked.

Nobody knew. They could all have been overboard long ago, and ought to have been. But they simply stood there without moving.

A turmoil broke out amidships. Something had happened. Three or four men were bawling at each other.

Let them bawl! The tumult spread. The first man jumped off the starboard side and smashed his head on the bilge keel. He had jumped short. And once again, dozens saw it.

Then something incredible, something fantastic happened.

'Fall in!' bellowed a voice. It was no joke. 'Fall in!' , someone roared. 'Get a move on, don't stand around like stuffed dummies. Fall in three deep. Get moving, gentlemen. We've no time to lose!'

They formed up as ordered and stood in three ranks, as though on the barrack square. As though they were on parade, not about to take a leap that meant life or death.

The tumult died away, stilled by the sudden command. The *Bismarck's* surviving ratings formed up three deep. During these last minutes the young seamen carried out orders as though on the parade ground, dressed by the right, faced Lieutenant-Commander Junack, faced the raging sea which in a few moments would receive them all, and one of them stepped forward and saluted.

Once more the sun broke through the overcast. It shone into pale, grimy faces; for many, for most of them, it was shining for the last time. A breaker came swirling over the deck. The men held on to one another. The last two or three files reacted too slowly and were swept prematurely into the sea.

'They've done it,' muttered a seaman in the second rank.

'Shipmates,' began the Lieutenant-Commander. 'We have done our duty. We have fought to the last. We must abandon ship. The first charges have been detonated... That's nothing to worry about. You have several minutes in hand. Don't jump short. Keep afloat as long as you can. Check your life-jackets again. Take your time.'

Between four and five hundred men stood there waiting for the next breakee, staring at the blazing ship, the oil patches in the water, the churning waves, the man next to them. As they waited for the final command they looked at the nearby British ships, which would perhaps pick them up if they managed to keep afloat long enough.

Now, at the last second of this parade, at the moment of doom, they performed the scene, they had so often rehearsed.

The Lieutenant-Commander raised his voice.

"Atten-shun! Three Sieg-Heils for our Fatherland! Long live Great Germany!'

'Sieg-Heil, Sieg-Heil, Sieg-Heil!'

They shouted as loud as they could. Their voices gave them courage, or at least a substitute for courage. That was all Lieutenant-Commander Junack had hoped to achieve by this last depairing gesture, this final act of defiance.

'Dismiss!' he commanded in a low voice.

That was the order for the death leap...

The boldest ventured first. They climbed up the steeply canted deck, grasped one another's hands, gave a shout, crouched down and jumped. Twenty-five to thirty feet down. Some were lucky, some unlucky. To be lucky meant to get away for the moment, to be unlucky meant to die. The bilge keel spelt death to many.

The second wave jumped. Petty officers helped Lieutenant-Commander Junack, who was driving the men into the sea with gentle encouragement or brutal orders.

'Come on. Don't spend so long thinking about it. It's your only chance.'

'I'm not going,' shouted Pollack.

'Oh yes, you are,' Lindenberg roared at him. 'You'll go, even if I have to kick you over.'

'I can't. Just look down there.'

'Look away, you cowardly bastard.'

Some four hundred were still on board, watching the perilous flight wide-eyed. The first men overboard were now twenty to thirty yards away. They waved, called out, then' swallowed water and spat it out, coughing and spluttering.

The men still on board saw that most of those already over the side were still alive, for the moment anyhow, and followed their example without further hesitation. Many shouted as they jumped, others closed their eyes or prayed. Sometimes two or three jumped together, holding hands, as though contact with a ship-mate could preserve them from the fatal bilge keel.

Again a breaker carried away six or seven men. Many were just waiting for this. A few made another attempt to jump from the wrong side. They were hurled against the hull by the swell until they lost consciousness and drowned. One or two were thrown back dead on to the *Bismarck*, as though the sinking ship was loth to let them go.

It was Lindenberg's turn. He had laboured like a berserker, encouraging and yelling at the others, and he hoped he still had a remnant of the fortitude he had been displaying during the last few minutes. He crawled up the sloping deck to the rail, waited for a couple of seconds, swore and shut his eyes. No, he must keep his eyes open.

The important thing was not to get away alive, but simply to jump and set the others an example. Perhaps the most merciful death was to be smashed against the steel side. It would certainly be quicker. What had the others gained by the fact that they were now drifting in the sea? How long could they hold out? Who would bother his head about them? A slow death is worse than a quick one... Pull yourself together, man, he told himself. Take a swing. Legs first. Not the left leg, that's unlucky. Right leg in front. Now! The ship will blow up at any moment.

The others were looking at him. The man on his left was down, now the one on his right was jumping. He also managed it successfully. It didn't look so bad. There, even Pollack was in the water. What a face he was making. Was he laughing or crying? How could Lindenberg tell, and what did it matter?

He straightened up, standing stiffly. His legs felt dead. All right, then he must jump with dead legs. He swung himself and jumped. He had a queer feeling in his back, as though he was on the giant dipper. Splash. Water. Waves. He made swimming movements and rose to the surface.

What an idiot I am, thought Petty Officer Lindenberg, there's nothing to it.

In the ice-cold water he felt hot. It whipped up his will to live, just as it later put it to sleep.

Lindenberg stared at the *Bismarck*. He watched Lieutenant-Commander Junack jump overboard, one of the last to do so. To his amazement the flag was still flying. What was happening to those still on board? Two more jumped off.

The wreck was filling all the time. It was heeling farther and farther over to port. It would go under at any moment now. Astonishing the punishment it had stood up to.

What was that he saw? Impossible! But of course that was how it had to be.

Captain Lindemann was clearly visible in his white cap as he stood erect on his sinking ship. Three men stood beside him. A great breaker poured across the deck. Lindemann hung on. The man on his left was swept overboard.

The Captain straightened up again, put his hand to his white cap in salute, saluted his men drifting in the sea, faced about and saluted the flag.

The men beside him were arguing with him. There could be no mistake about that. The Captain shook his head. He worked his way forward from the stern, past fires and over dead bodies, accompanied by two men. Once again he saluted his shipmates in the water.

That's absurd, thought Petty Officer Lindenberg. That's crazy. It's like on the films.

No, it wasn't a film. It was war. Not an actor, but a ship's captain.

Petty Officer Lindenberg could follow it all perfectly. So could dozens of his shipmates. There could be no mistake about what was happening. The two men who had stayed with the Captain were begging him to leave the ship. Lindemann refused. Then the men took matters into their own hands. They seized hold of him and tried to drag him overboard by force. He put up a desperate resistance. He struck out. He bellowed. Broke free. Returned to the quarterdeck. Saluted again.

Then came the end. The ship heeled over to port. Slowly, gradually, as though to give the men drifting near the hull a last chance to get away before it sucked them under. Then she suddenly turned bottom up.

Another few seconds and the hull sank. The screws were still turning. They were the last to disappear. It was all over. The biggest and most modern battleship in the world was gone, sunk by her own hand. With her went dozens, perhaps hundreds of her crew, who had not got off in time. With her went her Captain. With her went the flag.

The British watched the terrible scene spellbound. Their last torpedoes must have struck home. They closed in. They watched the German sailors jumping overboard as the ship sank deeper and deeper and finally turned slowly over on to her side. Admiral Tovey signalled to London the announcement that half an hour later was all over the world:

'*Bismarck* sunk.'

The British had no means of knowing that their torpedoes had done no damage whatever, that the new chrome-nickel armour plating was stronger than any torpedoes they had at that time. The bulk of the battleships were already homeward bound. At 10.20 a.m. the *Dorsetshire* fired two torpedoes. They exploded on the *Bismarck*'s starboard side. The last torpedo was fired at

10.36, from a range of 2,500 yards. It hit the port side. At 10.40 a.m., British Double Summer Time, the *Bismarck* sank.

For the British the battle was over. The sailors threw their caps in the air and shouted 'Hurray!' Everyone who could, left his action station, although no permis-sion to do so had been given, but victory and the re-laxation of tension automatically eased discipline. Everyone stared at the sinking *Bismarck*.

The sea carried the survivors towards the *Dorsetshire*.

Some five to six hundred men. Five or six hundred out of 2,402. The cruiser couldn't pick them all up. She radioed the *Maori* for assistance in the rescue work.

The destroyer was on the point of turning, when the sailors saw a man floating in the water. They called to him but he made no sign. They shouted again. Then he waved feebly. The shipwrecked man must be utterly worn out.

The *Maori* hove to, threw out a line and rescued the man. It was a Lieutenant-Commander who had been blown overboard by the blast from a shell, one of the first to go – it was Werner Nobis. He immediately lost consciousness again. They tore off his protective clothing, hosed him down, cleaned his oil-covered skin with petrol to open the pores, shook him till he came round and gave him brandy.

He smiled gratefully while still unconscious. He heard voices, voices in English, which he spoke fluently, but he couldn't understand a word.

He was taken into the sick-berth.

He was not alone there for long.

At first they drifted in a great mass. Then the sea swept them further and further apart. One or two had found a spar or one of the few still floating rafts and hung on to it. But the very effort to hold fast to these things tired them out earlier than the rest. One after the other they gave up exhausted and sank.

The sea hurled them this way and that, lifted them up, dragged them into whirlpools, washed over them, swirled them together, living and dead, wounded, despairing and dying. The icy water made them stiff with cold. The everlasting up and down, this way and that, paralysed their instinct of self-preservation, the last remnant of almost futile hope. The air-filled head-rest of the life-jackets pressed on the backs of their necks, pushing their heads further and further under water. A U-boat later sighted hundreds of drowned sailors who had lost the battle with his devilish head-rest. As a result of the observations reported by this U-boat, the life-jackets were altered. But that didn't help the crew of the *Bismarck*.

Would they be fished out? Would the enemy save them? Would he take the time to do so? Would he show that much humanity? Of course he will, the men told themselves: the Tommies are enemies, but they are still human beings. Their eyes were smarting with salt water. They could scarcely see. It was getting darker. Many lacked the strength to spit out the horrible sea water. Others drifted straight into the puddles of oil and put up one last desperate struggle.

Where were the enemy ships? They were there a moment ago. In fact the *Dorsetshire* and the *Maori* hove-to at exactly the spot to which the shipwrecked men were drifting. It was only a few hundred yards more. Those in front could already see the ships, tried desperately to hold course, lost it, were once more swept towards the silhouette, struck out and swam with their last remaining strength.

Leading Seaman Flieger was lying on his back, when he was startled by a cry from the man beside him. It took him several minutes to get his eyes open. He had been carried to the edge of a patch of oil, from which he just managed to escape. But the greasy stuff had gummed up his eyes. What luck, he thought. I'm being carried in exactly the right direction. The water washed over him, he lay back. Keep calm, he told himself, save your strength, move as little as possible, wait. Out of hundreds of shipmates Fate chose a few to escape with their lives.

Flieger shut his eyes. It was worst so close to the goal. My God, he thought, supposing I'm swept past, supposing I haven't the strength to hang on to the line. There was no chance of swimming back in that swell. He mustn't look. In the face of hope, the dread of death grows to measureless proportions.

Calm! Don't think about it. Think of something else. What month is it? May, of course, 27 May, 1941. The syringa was in flower, so was the lilac. It must be Mother's Day soon. What were they doing at home? They were bound to be thinking of him. What a good thing they didn't know what was going on. The papers would never tell the true story. Their families would never learn how many times their husbands and sons had died. The papers would trot out stupid, empty, worn-out phrases about heroism, fighting to the last shell, Great Germany and Faithful till Death. Of course, what else could they say?

They all wanted to be faithful till death, certainly, but when they made up their minds to it, when they swore it in youthful optimism, full of confidence in themselves, their nation, their fatherland, they didn't know what it meant.

Now they knew. The only thing that mattered now was to tell the others, to shout to them: Stop the war! Stop the thousandfold murder, put all those who want war on the *Bismarck* and let them perish there!

It was all useless. As long as there were human beings some would wallow in these phrases and the rest would be left to wallow in the sea.

He must hold out. Perhaps there was some way of escape. For Leading Seaman Flieger, at least. There must be.

To escape meant to see Marianne again, the tall blonde girl whom a smile suited so well, who sat day after day in the box office at the cinema, waiting for him. Manfried Flieger had discovered her on his last leave. He saw the film three times and each time he bought his ticket with a beating heart, just so that he could speak to her. He felt inhibited. The bluff seamanly approach seemed out of place here, although he was wearing a uniform. His voice sounded cracked. He wanted to tell her straight away that it was quite different with him. But naturally his thoughts were more nimble than his words. So he only asked if he could call for her when the cinema shut. She looked at him quizzically for a few seconds. Then she said, 'All right.'

It was more than he could have hoped for. He took her to an ale-house, because everything else was shut.

They sat facing one another for the first time. They smiled at each other. They understood each other without high-sounding phrases. They, too, used high-sounding phrases, but not until much later, when happiness simply wrung the words from them. They had found one another. And they had three days in front of them. Then it would become a service-post love like millions of others, but they believed in their love and meant to stay together, for ever.

For ever? No, he mustn't think about that. Again a wave whirled him round. Manfried Flieger felt something pressing on his neck. Two hands were clutching at him with a last burst of energy. A shipmate was holding on to him from behind. Perhaps without even knowing what he was doing. Both of them went down into the depths.

Flieger struck out wildly, rose to the surface and tried to drag the man's dead weight up with him, but he couldn't manage it. If he didn't break free from the other they would both drown. He swallowed water and spat it out. The other man seemed to have the strength of five. The situation was desperate.

'Let go!' roared Flieger.

But in his terror of dying the man only clung tighter. Flieger had to free himself. He acted at once, without stopping to think, without compunction, in obedience to the merciless instinct of self-preservation. He hit out as fast as he could, as hard as he could, again and again, striking the head of the other man, his shipmate. He saw the horrified, contorted face, the crazy, staring eyes, he felt sick, sick at himself, but he had no alternative. He had to act like this, even if he could never forget it for the rest of his life, even if those eyes appeared to him night after night. The drowning man's strength ebbed, his ha'nds released their grip.

Flieger dared not look at his shipmate, whose fate was now sealed, sealed by himself.

The first twenty or thirty of the shipwrecked had reached the port side of the *Dorsetshire*. When the lines were thrown over there were terrible scenes. Those behind forced their way forward. Four or five men grabbed a rope and hung on like grim death. One prevented the other from being saved. A few clear-headed men shouted. But what was the use of that, who listened, who took any notice? Comradeship, which had held firm for so long, now snapped. Every man for himself. And the salvation of one man might – mean death for another.

A few British sailors were leaning over the rails shouting down. They were doing what they could. They actually succeeded in hauling up a rope with. three men clinging to it. It moved slowly, very slowly. The others watched, stared. Quick, they must be quick, more and more of the survivors were reaching the *Dorsetshire*, and what use were a dozen ropes for three or four nundred men?

Suddenly the rope parted. The three men fell into the water, went under, rose to the surface shouting and blocked the way for the others.

All of a sudden Pollack floated up, yelling like a berserker.

'Let me go first,' he shouted. 'Let me go up. I've got a wife and child, don't forget that.'

It was no use. Pollack went on shouting.

Think of my wife and child.'

'Everyone here has a wife and child,' Lindenberg roared at him.

At last Pollack managed to get hold of a rope. The British sailor at the other end saw him and immediately hauled the rope up. Another six feet and the Able Seaman, who three days ago had become a father, would be safe. Another two or three seconds.

Then his strength failed him. He let go and fell into the water. Another man spotted it, swam to the rope, took hold of it and was heaved up. While Pollack screamed, whimpered and sank gurgling before the other man's eyes. There was no help now for anyone who could not help himself.

Later the sailors remembered details like this, remembered men dying a few feet from salvation. They spoke of it diffidently, unable to grasp the miracle of their own escape.

Dozens drifted past the *Dorsetshire*. They screamed for help, beat wildly about with their arms in an attempt to evade certain death and were swept on by the lashing sea.

Leading Seaman Rzonca saw a free line hanging aft. He broke away from the mob. But another man beat him to it. Rzonca watched him hauled aloft. A wave picked Rzonca up and hurled him violently against the ship's hull. He felt the blow as though from far away. Whatever happens, I mustn't lose consciousness, he thought. They'll throw the line out again in a moment.

A few seconds more, then came the next wave. Another blow. There was the line. And already another man was hanging on to it. But a second line was let down just beside it. The men on board must have spotted him. He caught hold of it. God give me strength, he prayed, just enough strength to hold on for a few seconds. He gripped the rope. He felt the weight of his body dragging him down, more and more forcibly. He could hold on no longer. His strength was exhausted. He was on the point of letting go.

But two British sailors leaned over, caught him under the arms and heaved him on board. He saw them grinning at him and passed out...

A few seconds later his pal Roemer was saved. A gigantic breaker raced towards the ship and poured over the deck, washing two or three men aboard and smashing dozens of others against her side.

The hellish struggle of the castaways went on. The yells, curses, moans and orders continued. Fifty hands continued to be stretched out for every rope. Men continued to be swept past to right and left, within a few yards of salvation.

How long would the British stick it? How long would they go on waving to the German sailors and shouting encouragement? How long would they go on toiling? How many would go on drifting in the sea for hours, before death released them?

Then it happened. Something horrible, monstrous. The death sentence for hundreds who might yet have been saved, whom the enemy was willing to save.

A German U-boat was spotted. Quite close to the *Dorsetshire*. A lookout reported a periscope. The alarm rang out.

'All hands to action stations!'

A few German submarines on their way back from a sortie had been ordered by the German Naval Command to intervene in the *Bismarck*'s fight to the death. But they had used up their torpedoes and were forced to look on helplessly as the already defenceless German flagship was pounded to a wreck and finally sank herself.

Now, without wishing to and without being able to avoid it, these U-boats pronounced the death sentence on their comrades of the *Bismarck*. The British had no means of telling that no danger threatened from the dreaded U-boats. They were bound to assume that in a few minutes, or even seconds, the deadly eels would be darting towards them.

'Full speed ahead!' came the order. 'Zig-zag course!'

But what in heaven's name was to become of the people still dangling from the ropes?

War at sea dictated the ghastly answer. The ropes were slashed, cut through. The shipwrecked men fell back into the sea with the useless rope's ends in their hands. At that moment they did not realize what had happened. They only realized that they must die – among them the young and courageous Petty Officer Lindenberg, who had just allowed a wounded man to be hauled to safety in front of him. Lindenberg was one of those who here, too, did more than their duty.

The *Dorsetshire* steered a fresh course. At full speed.

But the survivors' now futile cries for help died away among the churning waves of the Atlantic.

The sea took possession of them, consuming them by the hundred, the brave men who had been through hell. The grim, icy sea swallowed them up. Blindly and brutally, Fate entered their names in the lists of , the missing, turning wives into widows and children into orphans, wiping out differences of rank and making them all alike – cold and dead....

The same scene was enacted on the port side of the British destroyer *Maori*. Here, too, the lines were cut after the submarine had been sighted, here, too, the German sailors fell back into the sea with the rope's ends in their hands and cast a last despairing look at the enemy ship that had taken aboard a handful of their more fortunate shipmates. But they knew nothing of the German U-boats that had involuntarily brought the rescue to an end. Nor did they know that the British were making for base on their last drop of oil and for this reason, too, could spare no more time for picking up castaways.

Death paid its pimp, War, in the cash of human lives. ...

They died in clusters. Their cries for help grew less and less frequent.

Some shouted last words to one another, shook hands, embraced in the last struggle. They were seen hours later by ships passing the spot. Two of them were snatched from certain death by a U-boat shortly after midday.

For the rest it was all over by then. That's what they call a 'hero's death'...

Even as they waited for the U-boat to attack, the crews of the *Dorsetshire* and *Maori* took steps to save the lives of the German sailors provisionally rescued. Many were in danger of suffocation. Their life-jackets and oily clothes were whipped off and their naked, oil-covered bodies scrubbed with petrol. They were wrapped in blankets and shaken until they regained consciousness.

Oxygen was administered, stomachs were pumped out, brandy and whisky poured in, tablets, chocolate, cigarettes distributed. British sailors volunteered as blood donors.

There were eighty-three survivors aboard the *Dorsetshire*, thirty aboard the *Maori*. Almost half of them were still in immediate danger of dying – men who had swallowed fuel oil and could not breathe, who were suffering from heart attacks, had lost their sight or almost bled to death. The British did what they could.

They treated them as they would have treated their own men. When the ship's rations ran out, the sailors gave their own. On the *Dorsetshire* the whole crew was put on half rations. But the prisoners of war were allowed to eat whatever they would or could.

Nevertheless, there was one final panic on the *Maori*. The prisoners shouted and raced wildly about, tried to break out of the sick-bay, hit out and refused to let anyone touch them. One infected the other. The sick-bay staff did their best to quieten them. It was useless. The uproar grew worse and worse, more and more despairing – and yet every minute was vital, if the sick men were not treated at once many of them were bound to die.

The British Surgeon-Commander hurried through the ship. Perhaps the first man to be saved, a Lieutenant-Commander, who was fast asleep after a dose of sleeping tablets, might be able to calm his people down. The Surgeon-Commander shook Werner Nobis till he woke up.

It was some minutes before he came to.

'Do you speak English?' the Surgeon-Commander asked urgently.

'Yes, sir.'

'Will you do something to help me, please?'

'Of course,' replied Nobis.

'Your people must be got to sleep immediately,' the Surgeon-Commander went on. 'I wanted to give them a morphia injection, but they're afraid of me and turmoil has broken out. Give me a hand, quick.'

Nobis tried to stand up, but his legs gave way. The Surgeon-Commander supported him. Drunken with sleep, the German officer staggered to the sick-bay, where the uproar had meanwhile grown worse.

'Quiet, men!' he said. 'Be sensible. Nothing's going to happen to you. The Tommies are only trying to help you.'

'I'm not going to let them poison me,' sobbed a petty officer. 'They've already killed three men with injections.'

'Rubbish,' retorted Nobis roughly. He was almost overcome with exhaustion. He stopped and had to fight with all his will-power against his fatigue. 'Listen,' he went on, 'the ampoule contains morphia. A small dose, so that you can sleep. You'll wake up tomorrow feeling fine. Take my word for it.'

He exchanged a few words with the Surgeon-Commander in English, to show his people that he could talk to their captors. Then he collapsed. Two British sailors carried him back to his bunk.

The men calmed down at once. The survivors stared at the floor in embarrassment. The excitement of the last few hours had wrought havoc with their nerves. They were ashamed of themselves and wanted to explain it all to the British. They knew they had once again fallen victim to the propaganda that fed them day after day with stories of atrocities committed by the other side.

From now on everything went without a hitch. The men willingly stretched out their arms to the surgeon, smiling gratefully when he made the injection. The sick-berth contained thirty survivors from the *Bismarck* plunged in a deep, dreamless, healing sleep that lasted for ten to fourteen hours without a break. When they awoke they could not grasp the fact that they had escaped from the hell of war at sea, that the war for them was over...

For the British, who were still within range of the German *Luftwaffe* and U-boats, Operation *Bismarck* was not yet over. At 1 p.m. on this historic 27 May, 1941, the Reuter agency announced that the German flagship had been sunk. At 1.22 p.m. German Western Naval Command asked the Fleet Commander on the *Bismarck* for an exact statement of her position. In vain. The Bismack did not reply...

The great chase was ended. On the British side eight battleships and battle cruisers, two aircraft carriers, four heavy cruisers, seven light cruisers, twenty-one destroyers and six submarines had taken part in it. In addition numerous naval planes had flown sorties. All these forces in conjunction had succeeded in pounding the German flagship into a wreck, so that she had to sink herself. This did not entirely make up for the loss of the *Hood*, which had become a national idol...

After the *Bismarck* had already gone down, the British launched a final and now unnecessary attack by torpedo-carrying planes. Force H, Vice-Admiral Somerville's squadron, was too far from the *Bismarck* during the final phase of the engagement to intervene, yet close enough to hear the thunder of gunfire. Reports kept coming in to the effect that the destruction of the enemy was proceeding according to plan. The Vice-Admiral was therefore much perturbed to receive the following three signals in quick succession:

1. The *Bismarck* is still afloat;
2. Sir John Tovey's squadron cannot get her to sink by gunfire;
3. The battleships of this squadron are discon-tinuing the action through

lack of fuel.

Under these circumstances Sir James Somerville resolved to send the *Ark Royal*'s planes into action once more. Shortly after they had taken off the *Dorsetshire* at last radioed:

'*Bismarck* sunk.'

The torpedo planes were ordered to return. Since the rough sea made it dangerous to land with their torpedoes in place, they were forced to jettison them into the sea. Just after they had landed on the *Ark Royal* a twin-motor Heinkel in appeared and attacked the aircraft carrier, but missed its target.

Now Force H also put about and set course for Gibraltar, reaching the rocky fortress without mishap.

The Naval Staff sent out more destroyers to meet the returning British battleships. There were now eleven at sea. But it was a day and a half before they met and formed a unified squadron. A particular source of danger was the fact that the British units were compelled by their shortage of fuel to proceed at slow-speed.

On 28 May, a day after the sinking of the *Bismarck*, the long-feared assault by a powerful force of German bombers took place. Two destroyers, *Mashona* and *Tartar*, came under attack. *Mashona* was hit and sank. One officer and forty-five men were lost.

Thus ended the battle of the *Bismarck*.

During the night the survivors from the *Bismarck* fished out by the *Dorsetshire*, who now lay in a leaden sleep, were shaken awake. British sailors requested them in sign language to come to the sick-berth. Here lay three severely wounded men. Artificer Petty Officer Hauser who, after losing both his legs, had swum with indomitable will-power to the *Dorsetshire*, been hauled aboard and immediately operated on. He was in a state of severe delirium, but the British Surgeon-Commander was certain he would pull through. Beside him lay Engine-Room Artificer Schaefer, a living corpse, because he had swallowed so much fuel oil that he had to be artificially fed for the rest of his life. He is still alive.

But the present activity concerned the third man. It concerned Engine-Room Artificer Luettich.

'Does anyone speak English?' asked a British Sick Berth Petty Officer. 'Your shipmate is dying.'

The British went out of the room and left the Germans by themselves.

'Well, how are you?' asked Leading Seaman Rzonca.

His shipmates bent down to the mortally wounded Luettich.

'I shan't last much longer,' he answered in a low voice. He found it difficult to speak.

'Don't lose heart now, when the worst is over.'

A dozen men were standing round, trying not to let their feelings show in their faces. They stared at the first-aid cupboard and avoided looking at one another. They gritted their teeth. Each of them had met death a hundred times during the fighting. But then at least it was quick.

'I'm glad you're here...It's bad... when you're... alone.'

'We'll stay with you,' said Flieger soothingly. 'In a few days you'll be fine.' He tried to speak confidently, but his voice sounded brittle and thin.

'You'll... go... back home,' whispered the dying man, 'tell them... what... it was like.' Suddenly he tried to sit up, but fell back again. His voice was full of entreaty.

'Listen, don't spare them... tell them everything... tell them... just what it was like... tell the mothers... you must tell them... the wives... and... the children.'

His lips went on moving soundlessly. The white bandage round his head made his face look whiter still. Everyone could see the effort he was making to continue speaking, the way he painfully formed inaudible words and summoned up his last ounce of energy in an attempt to tell his shipmates something else before he died.

Some of them could bear it no longer. My God, they prayed, if it must be then let it be quick, give him a quick end, release him from his agony.

A few last words forced their way between the dying man's lips.

'It's... all... over. Cur... curse it... all.'

The Artificer was shaken by a convulsion. He groaned, shut his eyes, clenched his fists, then he moved no more, spoke no more, breathed no more.

'He's asleep,' said Flieger.

'Yes, he's asleep,' agreed 'Rzonca. 'Call the doctor, perhaps he can do something.'

The Surgeon-Commander appeared immediately. He bent down over the Artificer, raised his left eyelid with his thumb, straightened up sharply.

'Dead,' he said laconically. He shook hands with the group of Germans. He looked past them. His eyes were glistening.

Then he quickly left the room...

Each one took a last look at his dead shipmate, murmured a prayer and walked silently away.

The funeral took place at 10 a.m. the following morning. All the British sailors not on watch formed a square on the upper deck round their dead foe. He was sewn up in a sheet of sailcloth round which were wrapped the German colours. The white ensign flew at half mast.

An officer stepped forward and said the Lord's Prayer in English. The Commander made a short speech. Although very few of the German prisoners of war understood what he was saying, every one felt moved. Then the officer asked one of the dead man's shipmates to say a few words.

A petty officer stepped hesitantly forward.

'Dear dead shipmate,' he began. Then the words stuck in his throat. He began again. He wept, tried to recover his voice, looked at his comrades, then at the British, who were presenting arms before their dead enemy, at their grave young faces in which sympathy was clearly mirrored.

'We shan't forget you,' said the petty officer in a low voice.

The Commander gave a sign. The dead man was lowered into the water. One of the *Bismarck*'s crew played on a mouth organ borrowed from a British sailor *Ich hatt' einen Kameraden* – 'I had a comrade'.

Then they stood – eighty-two men who had come through alive. Their thoughts dissolved in tears, their bodies were convulsed with sobs – and they asked themselves, what is it all for, what's the use of it, for whom, against whom?

They could give themselves no answer.

In the sea, a few yards from the hull of the British cruiser, a bundle enveloped in the German colours sank to a sailor's grave.

The German High Command announced the *Bismarck*'s loss at once. The way was prepared for the imminent disaster by the report of a major naval engagement some four hundred sea miles west of Brest.

The newspapers, which had just been celebrating the victory over the *Hood*, had now to describe the end of the *Bismarck*. No details were given. Not a word about the inadequate preparations that had preceded the German squadron's break-out into the Atlantic, not a word about the fact that the enterprise was from the outset labelled 'Victory or Death'.

The press quickly changed the subject. The Ministry of Propaganda did not want any discussion of the *Bismarck*'s voyage of death. Only the thousands of re-lations, mothers, wives and children, continued to talk about it. They never got over it.

They never again saw their husbands, fathers and sons who went down on the edge of the Bay of Biscay in the Atlantic.

The survivors from the *Bismarck* slowly came to themselves, slowly recovered from the shock. Gradually cigarettes began to taste good again and the men no longer sat in a corner staring into space. They began to talk freely to one another again. For the most part they were allowed to move about the ship at will. They went up on deck to get fresh air and looked silently out over the endless waste of water, in which their friends and comrades had ended their sufferings.

Then, all of a sudden, war at sea was with them again. Air-raid warning on the *Maori*. Heinkel 111s. Carpet bombing. British anti-aircraft fire. Bombs close overside. Hits. Explosions. Yells. Wounded. A list. Curses. Fear.

Would it never end? Having escaped a tiny fraction of the holocaust, must they now tremble before their own bombs?

The *Maori* got away, severely damaged.

Alarm bells on the *Dorsetshire*. A German U-boat sighted. Full-speed on a zig-zag course. When would the torpedoes come? When would they once more hear the command. Abandon ship!

The men sat below decks. Once more their eyes wavered. Once more some fell silent while others talked too much. But this time they were lucky. The *Dorsetshire* reached port without loss of life.

The German officers got their men together.

'We shall now be interrogated,' said Lieutenant-Commander Junack. 'You know the rules of the Geneva Convention. You don't have to make a statement. But one thing is most important. Under no circumstances must you tell the Tommies that we sunk the *Bismarck* ourselves. Understand?'

'Aye-aye, sir,' replied a petty officer, 'but why should we let them think they did it?'

'That's quite simple,' answered the officer. 'They needn't know that our armour plating was stronger than their torpedoes.'

No sooner do we get away from the war than we're thinking about the war again, reflected Rzonca bitterly. But he said nothing. It was not until after the war that British intelligence officers learnt that the German flagship had been scuttled.

Now they had time to write. They didn't know when they would see their families again, but now they had escaped certain death they could at least hope that one day they would see them. After the war. In peace. After a time that must never come again...

Lieutenant-Commander Nobis made a quick recovery. As a friendly gesture the British had given him an officer's cabin on the *Dorsetshire*. To begin with, they asked him no questions. Officers came to visit him, left cigarettes and chocolate on the locker, were surprised by his perfect English and occasionally yarned about the good old days in the merchant navy.

Nobis soon managed to look objectively at the hell he had passed through. He knew what a wretched employer he had given his services to. He knew the duty he had now to assume. He would tear the mask from the face of war, he would describe the great holocaust in the *Bismarck* as it was – without embellishment, without patriotic trimmings, without inflated phrases.

When he was in Portugal and had an opportunity of turning his back on war, he voluntarily made his way back to Germany. In spite of Deina. War had let him go, one of the 116 it allowed to escape. And nowthathe had escaped from the slaughter and was no longer a henchman of the murderer war, the future seemed to him clear and simple. One day the war would come to an end. And he would be free and able to go back to Deina. And one day there would be peace...

Forever?

An Englishman gave Nobis writing paper and a pen and without asking many questions agreed to post the German prisoner of war's letter to Deina. Nobis put everything down in black and white. The horror and futility of it all.

'Every word you said was right. I have paid for it, believe me, and I have cursed the madness that drove me away from you. Never again. Never again can there be any other duty for me than to love you. If you still want me to. If you still can let me.'

Werner Nobis didn't know whether his letter would reach Deina.

He told himself how little hope there was and at the same time he built on this hope. He was put ashore in England... And one day he heard his name called out during the distribution of post. He looked at the letter, saw the Portuguese postmark and he held it in his hand for several minutes, not daring to open it.

Then he read it. Deina's answer was simple, clear and to the point. She wrote exactly what he had hoped she would, in spite of everything. The last sentence read:

'One day the war will be over, and then....'

Lieutenant-Commander Junack also wrote, to his fiancée in Hamburg. After the war he went back and married her. Rzonca married by proxy while still a prisoner of war. In 1943. For four years the marriage existed only on paper. Then he went home. Soon his son Friedrich came into the world, and in 1952 Rzonca went to sea for the last time – emigrating to America...

How did the other survivors of the *Bismarck* fare in captivity? They had fallen into the hands of an enemy who played the game. They remained in England for a few months and were then taken across to Canada. Two years later, in 1943, Able Seaman Braun and Flieger played a trick on their guards that got into all the papers...

A few hundred men were interned in a camp near Monthis. The war seemed as though it would never end. Post came regularly. The food was excellent. But no one likes living behind barbed wire. For weeks Braun and Flieger, who had been fished out of the sea by the *Dorsetshire* side by side two years ago, had been planning escape.

Now the time had come. They had got hold of a bucket of paint and a couple of painter's overalls. Braun had grown up in Canada and spoke the language fluently. He had taught the essentials to his friend Flieger. They painted the posts of the camp from the inside. Then they went to the gate. It was unsuspectingly open for them. The guards did not take their jobs too seriously. Who could escape from Canada? They painted two or three posts from the outside. Then they threw away the ladder and ran across country as fast as they could go.

They got away. They had managed to scrape some money together. Braun bought two suits. Nobody suspected him. Now they were free men. But freedom calls for money. They found jobs as waiters. No one asked for papers. They were doing fine. A few hours' work a day and payment in money that still had some value. The whisky was good and when they were through for the day their Canadian girl friends were waiting for them. They found a nice flat. Their neighbours raised their hats to them.

Then the blow fell. A ludicrous coincidence put them behind barbed wire again. Every time they served a meal they passed through a little ante-room on their way to the kitchen. Here stood a plate of sandwiches for the waiters. There were a dozen of them working in the big restaurant. Waiters are always in a hurry. They were therefore in the habit of snapping up a sandwich as they passed through the ante-room. They would take a bite out of it and carelessly throw the rest down anywhere. Canada was a land of plenty, even in wartime. Such wastefulness shocked the two escaped prisoners of war. Their German instinct for efficiency somehow couldn't stomach it. They got hold of a plate on which to put the sandwiches they had taken a bite from, so that they could pick them up again next time and eventually finish them. In this way they wasted nothing.

This behaviour caught their colleagues' eye. There's something fishy about those two, they told one another. They can't be real Canadians. One of the other waiters went to the police – and Braun and Flieger became prisoners of war again.

At the beginning of 1947 the last prisoners from the *Bismarck* were released. The survivors were dumb-founded by the long-awaited miracle of the return home. Most of them went to sea for the last time – on the homeward voyage.

The *Bismarck* brought the German Navy its proudest victory and its most agonizing defeat. A warship, a miracle of technology that stood up to every test and yet went down and took with it thousands of despairing, anguished, courageous seamen. They put to sea with laughing faces and they died with their faces twisted in agony. Their death struggles lasted for days or hours, and at the end they were left to themselves, without escape, without hope, without consolation. They watched their shipmates die and knew their turn would come soon. They drifted in the water, had the lines thrown out by the British already in their hands... and nevertheless they had to die, this time for good. The sea swallowed them up.

On charts a simple cross marks the spot at which the *Bismarck* sank. The families of her crew wept and hoped, hoped futilely, still hope even now. In their death all the men of the *Bismarck* had left was the traditional motto 'Faithful till Death'. They did not Invent it. But' they had to obey it and they had to leam what obeying it meant. It became their death sentence. They saw their own blood flowing across the wet deck plates. They experienced both the miracle of comradeship and the brutal outbursts of the instinct of self-preservation. They died alone or in groups. They went down cursing or praying, despairing or apathetic.

And the slogan that brought them death, that was printed in the newspapers, that is hammered into young German recruits when they take the oath, that cost hundreds of thousands, millions of human lives – 'Faithful till Death' – became their last curse, their last consolation, their final delusion.